The Way to Life

THE WAY TO LIFE

Sermons in a Time of World Crisis

by

HELMUT GOLLWITZER

translated by
David Cairns

T. & T. Clark
36 George Street, Edinburgh

Contents

Note by the Translator

It has been suggested by the Publisher that some information about Professor Gollwitzer's life should be given. On my invitation he has supplied the following material. "Born 29th December 1908, in Pappenheim, Bavaria, the son of a Protestant minister. Classical Grammar School education till 1928; thereafter studied Protestant Theology and Philosophy in Munich, Jena, Erlangen and Bonn, especially under Paul Althaus, Friedrich Gogarten, and Karl Barth; 1932 First Theological Examination, Doctor of Theology, Basel, 1937; 1934–5 Domestic Chaplain in Austria, 1936–7; worked with the Council of Brethren of the Confessing Church in Thüringen; 1937 forbidden by the Gestapo to speak in public, 1937–8 theological worker with the Prussian Council of Brethren; 1938–40 representative of Martin Niemöller in his parish Berlin–Dahlem after his imprisonment; September 1940 expelled from Berlin and forbidden by the Gestapo to travel; 1940 conscripted for military service; 1941 at his own request a medical orderly in France and Russia; 1945–50 prisoner of war in the Soviet Union; 1950–57 Professor of Systematic Theology and Protestant Theology in the Theological Faculty of Bonn University; from 1957 Professor in the Philosophical Faculty of the Free University of Berlin; retired since 1975. Honorary Doctorate of Theology of Heidelberg University, Doctor of Divinity, Glasgow University and Aberdeen University."

Those who wish to know more about Dr. Gollwitzer's background should read his moving story of his imprisonment in Siberia, where he worked in the asbestos mines. This book was published in an English translation by the S.C.M. Press, London, in 1953 under the title "Unwilling Journey".

In these sermons there are a number of topical references, most of which are self-explanatory. There is, however, one reference to Undine Zühlke, Cornelius Burkhardt, and Bishop Scharf (on pages 26 and 31) which requires some elucidation. Here again, Professor Gollwitzer has given some help for foreign readers. He writes: "In the autumn and winter of 1974–5 there were violent disputes because the Springer Press, which dominates the market, made sharp attacks on the authorities and pastors of the Protestant Church. The reason for this was that the Bishop of Berlin, Kurt Scharf, had, for pastoral reasons, visited adherents of the terroristic Red Army Faction who were in Berlin prisons, and two Church workers, a pastor's wife and prison visitor Undine Zühlke, and a curate Cornelius Burkhardt, had tried to establish communication between these prisoners and their sympathisers, after the murder of the President of the Superior Court von Drenkmann, in order to prevent further activities of this kind by a terrorist group.

For this they were themselves arrested on the charge of conspiring with terrorists, and subjected to a wearisome legal investigation, although their innocence was obvious from the beginning."

The passages of Scripture quoted at the head of the sermons are taken from the Revised Standard Version, with the exception of Sermon 16, where use is made of the Authorised Version, for reasons will be obvious to the reader.

February, 1981.   David Cairns.

Foreword

Preaching, a singular form of speech, developed from its earliest days by the Christian Church to hand down the history of the great hope, the history of Israel and its God, the history of Jesus of Nazareth, the history of the spiritual explosion of the Resurrection Community. It is not the only form of speech for this transmission; conversation, discussion, tableau, ritual formulae and words interpreting actions, stand beside it as of equal value, and today are more popular with many.

Anyone who in spite of the great tradition, or because of it, commits himself to it, and does so actively, as himself a preacher, will find out that in no other form of speech are things taken so seriously, is our whole existence so challenged, even put at risk. In no form of speech does our word itself so much take the form of action, of intervention in the history of the hearers, as in this. Perhaps there is one exception here, the conversation between two people which in church circles is commonly known as pastoral conversation, in which it is not necessary for an official pastor to participate, or for a religious word to be spoken, in which life-decisions are made, and in which both participants hope that the one may speak a word of truth, of judgement, and of help to the other.

These two situations involving speech, the most intimate confidential dialogue between two persons, and the wholly public situation of preaching, are the two most momentous that I know, both of them calling for the most serious reflection, for the disregard of all subsidiary interests, especially all thoughts of vanity, all striving for effect, all thought of private profit. These are situations demanding liberation from self, and therefore to be faced only in prayer, in prayer for such liberation.

The theological movement of the nineteen-twenties which inspired me at the beginning of my theological studies, and enduringly influenced my life, was marked by an awareness of the seriousness of the preacher's situation. The theoretical expression which was found for it often sounds very authoritarian to modern ears, as a ministerial ideology which unduly exalts pulpit language as something superhuman. But we rightly understand the urge to distinguish it from psychology, aesthetic and rhetoric, when we realize that the motive behind it was the discovery which had previously been almost forgotten – the discovery that in the preaching situation something vital is at stake, just as vital as in the most intimate conversation leading to decision. Of this both the speaker and the hearer should be aware.

As a way to secure the freedom required if preaching is to be taken seriously, my friends and teachers – here I have especially to name Karl Barth, Eduard Thurneysen and Hermann Diem – recommended in the Reformed tradition text-sermons, that is, the attachment of the sermon to a biblical text. They taught that the Bible text should not be merely a motto placed at the head of the sermon, not merely the occasion for all sorts of associations, not merely a peg on which to hang a theme chosen by the preacher, but should be in concrete control of the preacher. The sermon should make this text more perspicuous to the hearer than it was before. At the same time it should give pleasure, so that one is thankful for it, and be a source of guidance for life today. The preacher's subordination to this text frees him from all other authorities, from ecclesiastical authorities – that was the liberating experience of the Reformation – and from political authorities – that was the liberating experience at the time of Hitler's dictatorship.

For this reason my sermons to this day have always been sermons from a text, and perhaps this makes them sound rather old-fashioned to younger theologians. I wonder at their preference for handling themes, in the service of which the biblical text is then exploited, and do not know whether I ought to admire the courage that is needed to believe that one's own ideas have so much truth-content in them that people should use Divine Worship to expound them. For it is, after all, that same gathering of the congregation, which should equip it, by the handing down of the great story of hope, to be a living cell in the world of men that is being shaken by deadly convulsions. But there can be no law ordaining that sermons should have a text, everyone must see what authorizes him to open his mouth in the name of the living God, and we can only tell each other what helps us to face up to the moment of truth which is the hour of public worship.

In my experience, subordination to the biblical text has a liberating effect also because in this moment of truth which challenges our responsibility to an unusual degree, it sets us free from responsibility for what is to be said here and now. The text takes over the responsibility, and through it, he in whose name these first witnesses spoke, to whom we owe our biblical texts. If I had to preach my convictions, my knowledge, and my experiences, what fills my heart at the present moment, and what stirs my mind, my Christianity and the certainty of my faith, then the responsibility would wholly lie with me, and the question whether I am at this precise moment a believer, and am certain of all these astonishing assertions of the Christian faith, might rightly hinder me from putting my foot on the first step of the pulpit stairs. What makes me go on, and open my mouth, can only be the knowledge that I have not to speak out of the wealth of my religiosity, but rather that I, a poor doubting man, am the first hearer of what the ancient text proclaims and promises to me and to all who sit before me. What is said to me, and what I have to pass on to others, is always much more than what I could say on my own authority, much more than I have already experienced, know, and believe. It is always something unbelievable, incomprehensible, inconceivable, that is now to be proclaimed, and something through which in our company, including the preacher as well as the hearers, new beginnings of hope, new hope for beginners, and consequently discipleship of beginners must come into being.

Today we have been compelled to rediscover the inseparability of faith and discipleship, faced by the challenges of a murderous century, and through Christian self-criticism in the knowledge of Christian failure in the past and the present due to the separation of faith and discipleship. Discipleship becomes a reality in time, in this present time and in all spheres of life. Through discipleship faith becomes political. For this reason submission to a text from distant times does not remove us from this present age of ours, and least of all when the text is asked what it says to men today about faith as discipleship, as it once said to the men of its own time. Its relationship to its own times illuminates its relationship to our times today, and vice versa. For this reason preaching, which aims at faith as discipleship stands, just because concentrated attention is paid to the text, at one and the same time "between the Bible and the newspapers" as the young Barth put it in a letter to Thurneysen. What the newspaper brings is not to be discarded, but to be included, for it makes us acquainted with the living material and the conditions of a life of discipleship. It acquaints us with the challenges, the questionings, our faith has to meet, and the situations in which it is tested. For this faith the great history of hope empowers us, invites us, and rouses us. For this reason preaching can never be more than the fresh beginning of the permanent conversation within the congregation about contemporary faith and contemporary discipleship. Not a conclusive word, but always a rousing and stimulating word, seeking for amplification, correction, and continuation in the conversation of all its hearers with one another.

The text, and the great message which it contains are meant to be a source of joy. For this reason the hour of solemnity is not an hour of deadly, but of joyful solemnity, always an hour of celebration. A sermon is a speech of celebration in a company met together for celebration. It is surrounded and borne up by the festive utterances of the whole company. These are missing in the case of printed sermons, which is their loss. It is to be hoped that the reader can make good the defect from his own experience. All the sermons were preached in Christ Church in Dahlem.

Eastertide, 1980.   Helmut Gollwitzer.

Part One

Work that is Worthwhile

Now the whole earth had one language and few words. And as men migrated to the east, they found a plain in the land of Shinar and settled there. And they said to one another, "Come let us make bricks, and burn them thoroughly." And they had brick for stone, and bitumen for mortar. Then they said, "Come, let us build ourselves a city, and a tower with its top in the heavens, and let us make a name for ourselves, lest we be scattered abroad upon the face of the whole earth."

And the Lord came down to see the city and the tower, which the sons of men had built. And the Lord said, "Behold, they are one people, and they have all one language; and this is only the beginning of what they will do; and nothing that they propose to do will now be impossible for them. Come, let us go down, and there confuse their language, that they may not understand one another's speech." So the Lord scattered them abroad from there over the face of all the earth, and they left off building the city. Therefore its name was called Babel, because there the Lord confused the language of all the earth, and they left off building the city. Therefore its name was called Babel, because there the Lord confused the language of all the earth; and from there the Lord scattered them abroad over the face of all the earth. Gen. 11, 1–9.

A friend who is very near to me has asked me to expound some day the story of the building of the Tower of Babel; and I had intended to do this on the next Sunday that I have to preach here in Dahlem. Now this happens to be the Sunday after Labour Day, and therefore this seems really a quite specially suitable text. For here in this story too, men are working away, bricks are fired, and discoveries are made, e.g. how asphalt is got, and how also it can be used as mortar. A great endeavour unites the whole of mankind. And then everything is labour lost, then the result is the opposite of what men had worked for. "Then I considered all that my hands had done and the toil that I had spent in doing it, and behold, all was vanity, and a striving after wind; there was nothing to be gained under the sun," says the preacher Solomon. (Eccl. 2, 11). Whether that is *all* that is to be said about our human striving and building, about all the tower-building in human history, that will be our final urgent question. But one thing is certain, at least one of the things to be said is this: I must confess that the more I think about this old story, the more contemporary it becomes.

The whole history of German labour in this century is in this story. What an industrious, even work-mad people these Germans are! The whole world admires them for this, and we are proud because of this admiration. But what has in fact resulted from this work? At the beginning of the century we had decided to become a great Power, and we worked to this end, and because one cannot achieve this without strong armaments, we worked for armaments. Krupp's iron-foundry in Essen was the symbol of German labour. Then came the war, and in the war we slaved for the war. Then it came to reconstruction, and when the time of high unemployment came, people praised the Führer because he restored employment, But it was work for the Autobahns and for rearmament, work for war. Once more in the war we slaved for the war, and once again, after the collapse, we set about the work of reconstruction, and when that was achieved, there returned the spectre of unemployment. If we had not now the work for armaments, how the number of the unemployed would soar! Wherever protectors of the environment warn about a source of chemical poisons, or citizens take the initiative against an atomic power centre that threatens the future, or where protests make themselves heard against the folly of rearmament, – e.g. in the great demonstration in Bonn on the 22nd of May – there the great argument is always trotted out – the number of people employed. Even if it is only work that will lead to future destruction, the important thing is that it gives employment. Obviously we do not know a more reasonable use for our labour power than to set it to work for the destruction of our own future. So then this was the Babylonian rhythm of German labour in the twentieth century, work in preparation for war, war work, post-war work then again work in preparation for war, war work, post-war work – and now perhaps we are already in the middle of work in preparation for war, for many of the specialists in armament problems tell us, that the danger of a new war, an atomic war, is not decreasing but increasing, and that there is a great probability that our work today is once again nothing but work in preparation for war. This is all the crazier, since all the urgent problems of our time, world hunger, exploitation of raw materials, conservation of the landscape, the feeding and housing of the increasing world population, could easily be solved, if we were to make an end of the folly of squandering our work in arming: in terms of money, 300,000 million dollars per year. Nearly half all the scientists in the world, are working today at the further development of the weapons of death, and millions of workers and soldiers in addition.

That is the present, and how was it in the past? The building of the Tower of Babel is the history of the great Empires, from century to century the great Empires and their great Caesars. They unite many lands and peoples under their rule, *one* ruling language, *one* administration, *one* culture. All this happens in the name of union and peace, all, it is claimed, for the blessing of mankind – Pax Romana, Pax Germanica, Pax Britannica, Pax Americana. But when the unification reaches its culminating point, the decay has always already set in. There must be some kind of canker in these attempts at unification. And yet today we really need unification. Do you remember how, after 1945, after the end of the attempt to unite Europe under German domination, everybody spoke of world government, whose time had now come – and today mankind is as fragmented as ever it was, particularly today when really a common effort of will among all nations is necessary to end the madness of armaments, for a new world economic order, and for the saving of our biosphere if we do not wish to perish. Instead of that we hear today the despairing talk of the "ungovernable character of the world". In great matters as in small, in large-scale politics as in small groups, in town-councils and in Presbyteries, our work remains fruitless because we cannot understand ourselves, because it seems as if we were all speaking quite different languages, because what continually happens is like what is said here, that "no one any longer understood another man's language".

Thus the ancient narrator three thousand years ago described what he saw round about him when he looked at the great Empires of that time, Egypt and Babylon, and at the same time he predicted the history of mankind up to the present day. For this purpose he used a story which he did not himself invent, but which people were telling each other everywhere in the oriental world at that time, and by which they used to explain the origin of two quite different phenomena, the origin of tower-like mounds, or rather high towers and ruins of towers, which people gazed at with wonder in the Mesopotamia of that day – and the phenomenon of the many kinds of language, which are so troublesome because they make it hard for one man to understand another. The gods must have interfered here – hence these enigmatic mounds and ruined towers, and hence the confusion of the nations and languages.

The biblical narrator, who adopted this aetiological saga (that is what scholars call such stories about origins), has no concern for the gods, he does not believe that there live above us gods who feel jealous and anxious because of the great powers of man, and for that reason intervene in defence of themselves. He knows, as an Israelite, the one living God, the Creator, who loves his creatures, who has equipped his human beings with many gifts and great powers, who wills to bless their work and make it prosper, who rejoices in the powers of his creatures. And yet he sees a truth in this saga, and for that reason he places it at the end of his account of the beginnings of the history of mankind, which is now contained in the first eleven chapters of the book of Genesis. Thus a good beginning – the man and the woman in the garden of this earth, they have food and work, they live in peace and fellowship, the work is profitable, it is a healthy world. Then this one special, specially endowed creature of God – man, destroys more and more the Creation and himself, Adam and Eve, Cain and Abel, the men of the story of the Flood, and lastly this tower-building – these are the stages of an accelerating disorder, destruction growing like an avalanche which starts with men and turns back on themselves. The narrator merely tells the story; he does not comment on it. But his narrative forces this question upon us, what has gone wrong here, that man is so destructive, and that God does not bless men, but confronts them with his judgement?

Far too frequently we apply here the word "sin" that so easily comes to the lips of Christians. But have we any idea of what we mean by this, and how much it concerns us all? Not merely a few individual bad thoughts and actions, which could be avoided by making some moral effort, is what is meant here, but something destructive, which intertwines itself with even our best efforts, something that poisons not only

individual actions and individual people, but also great shared enterprise, orders of society, economic structures, and the structures of our
States. The people in our story aim at something quite good and
reasonable, they do not wish to be "scattered", to be removed far from
each other, and thus perhaps come into conflict and enmity; they wish
to remain together, they wish for a good common life, fellowship,
peaceful order. But the wrong note has already been struck *"that we
may make a name for ourselves"* is what they say. Ambition is here
named as a form of what is false and poisonous. The favourite activity
of the nations is to get on the merry-go-round of their own fame, said
once Friedrich Wilhelm Foerster, one of the most passionate, and
therefore the most abused critics of the Germans in our own century.
How true that is to our own experience! Vanity and the desire for fame
destroy the best work both in personal life and politics. Thus other
nations are oppressed because of our desire for greatness, and in our
own nation people must be oppressed by concentration camps and
mass executions. Here there is talk of fine achievements, of fellowship
within the nation, of unification and peace, but that merely disguises
the fact that some oppress and others are oppressed, that those who
have the upper hand live at the cost of the underdogs. Whether we
speak of the desire for glory or the lust of possessions, or the lust for
privilege – the desire of some to have it better than others – the
splendid aim of fellowship is always disintegrated and destroyed by the
egoism of individuals, of classes, and of nations, and the end result is
the opposite of the thing we have been working for. *"That we may not
be scattered"* this was what the work of unification began with, and
"they were scattered all over the face of the earth", that is the result.

Must this always be repeated? Is there not a way out of this story of
mankind's self-destruction? Is there not another way? This is today our
most urgent question, since today the catastrophe that threatens us is
not, like the previous one, one that could be survived, but a disaster
that we and our children and grandchildren will probably not survive.
It is our urgent question, because we see ourselves so chained to this
universal lust for fame and possessions, to the desire to live better at
the cost of others, and at the same time realize what this leads to. This
biblical narrator is, like all those in the Bible who speak with us, deeply
convinced that we cannot by our own power break our fetters, cannot
get rid of our intoxication, that we need another great help. The
Creator, who made the good beginning, must make a new beginning.
He must come with new gifts, in order that the old gifts of our abilities
and our work do not continue to be a curse to us. A new spirit must set
us free from the errors of our old spirit. The whole Bible is a cry for
help of this new Spirit from the Creator, and the whole Bible is at the
same time the *euangelion,* the glad news, that God does not only, as in
our story, confront the evil will of man with his judgement, but that he
has opened his heart to us, and made possible a new way of good life, of
fellowship, of avoidance of destruction. Into this new way he desires to
lead us all by his Spirit.

This story stands immediately before the story of Abraham's departure from the great kingdom of Babylon. Abraham – that is the new beginning of a new history, the new history of God, the history of healing for sick humanity. This new history again has as its stations Abraham – Israel the people that has a new bond with God and a new ordering of society – the prophets who call men back to this ordering of society, and ever and again make clear God's life-giving will – Jesus the presence of God in the midst of his people and in the midst of a confused and disrupted humanity – the forgiveness of the Cross and the light of the Resurrection: there the new way opens up, the "way of salvation" the "way of righteousness" the "way of truth", the "way of peace" thus it is spoken of in the New Testament with a wealth of new descriptions.

This way is a way of Exodus, as it was for Abraham, a way out of the Babylonian arrogance, ambition, and greed, and its methods of oppression and structures of oppression that destroy fellowship. To this way we are called, we are not merely invited, but have been apprehended by God's Spirit, and set upon it. Everyone of us has already had a few experiences of this kind. . . It is essential now that we should not depart from it, as we unfortunately do again and again. We must go forwards in the way of the new life against the old Babylonian way, and employ all our efforts in the service of the good life of men in fellowship, using God's gifts as God wishes them to be used, and daily letting ourselves be purified from the adulteration of our good efforts by ambition and greed – that is the work that may hope for blessing.

To some this will appear too modest an answer. This turning from the old way to the new way seems to happen only to some few people, but the nations, the ruling classes, the Governments – they all seem to be travelling along the old tracks; which today we see so clearly are leading to destruction. There are Christians who, in consequence of this, entirely withdraw themselves from the international problems within the boundaries of personal life and personal piety, and there are others who believe that faith cannot help us in international and social questions, that only the struggle for juster political policy can.

The narrator of our story does not agree with either of these positions. His faith does not make him turn aside from world history and world politics, but actually gives him insight, he does not "write the nations off", but is wholly concerned with the question how the fate, not only of individuals, but of the whole of humanity can be given a turn for the better. And, on the other hand, he does not feel that faith, our bond with God, because it is only the affair of individual men and small groups, can have no influence on public life. He sees mankind as wholly lost without God's help, but he sees God's help as already active and present, he sees it begin with individuals and small groups, and with God's promise he has vowed that from these small cells and centres a dynamic influence will have a large-scale effect. Whole societies can lose the taste for boasting, exploitation and oppression through the contagious influence of "Abrahamitic minorities" as Dom

Helder Camara puts it. That is no recipe to apply to all the questions
that oppress us today, but it is the beginning from which we can start.
To these small cells it may be our privilege to belong, and we can work
outwards for their influence upon our so severely threatened world.
That is the work which is worthwhile, and for which a blessing is
promised.

We bring today before you, O Lord and source of our life, the
urgency of our work; the many who have work, and whose work preys
upon them, or who suffer from its meaninglessness. You see what an
immense amount of work is spendthrift of body and spirit; what an
immense amount of work is wasted on frivolous or deadly purposes.
You see also the millions who have no work, who lose their self-respect
through unemployment, fall into need, or into ways of crime or dis-
ease, especially the young people who would like to learn to work and
are excluded from it. You see, Lord, our perplexity and feebleness, the
opposition to better solutions, and the conflicts of mankind that cry out
to heaven. We hear from your Gospel that you do not look down on
men with remote indifference, that you are present and active among
us, that you suffer with all sufferers, and that you wish to be a helper for
your humanity. So we pray for your helping Spirit for all who are
distressed by their work, and for all who are distressed because they
have no work. Show to each of us meaningful tasks to which he can
apply his gifts! Bless the work of those who wish so to alter the wrong
conditions that work may no longer be meaningless, and that no one
may be prevented from working. Take not from us your blessing,
which you have promised for all true work in the service of men! And
when you take us out of work through illness and old age, then let us
come to know that we do not live by our work, but by your grace! Let us
say "Yes" to rest as well as to work. May your grace be a light in
activity and in rest, in this earthly life and in that life above where we
will give thanks without end for your help!

The Sufferers' Quiet Song of Defiance

*God is our refuge and strength, a very present help in trouble. Therefore
we will not fear though the earth should change, though the mountains
shake in the heart of the sea; though its waters roar and foam, though the
mountains tremble with its tumult. There is a river whose streams make
glad the city of God, the holy habitation of the Most High. God is in the
midst of her, she shall not be moved; God will help her right early.*
Psalm 46, 1–6.

Lord our God, time and again you set us free when we are bound. The
Reformation too, four hundred years ago, was a liberation from tutel-
age and oppression by men, and distortion of faith by human supersti-
tions. It gave the freedom to hear you yourself in your word. Today
you ask "What use we are making of our freedom, what bondage
prevents us today from freely hearing you, and going your way?" Your
word wills to cut through all other bonds, and make us free for a new
life in the midst of men in bondage. But we love our fetters more than
your freedom. So we confess to you our enslavement to possessions, to prejudices, to hate, to unbrotherliness, to vanity, and
fear of your freedom. You became a brother to slaves in order to lead
them to freedom. Lord, we ask you to do that and to have pity on us!

I am now going to make a certain venture, and I ask you to cooperate
with me. It consists in this, that we should agree to consider the hymn
"A safe stronghold our God is still" – Luther's hymn, the Reformation
hymn which some of us perhaps today can hardly bring themselves to
sing. A venture, to sing it together on Reformation Sunday! In doing
this, how shall we keep clear of the wake of the tradition of this hymn?
How shall we avoid wallowing in the sentiment of the patriotic
Protestant swelling breast with which formerly male voice choirs
and student corps thundered out this hymn as a Christian and
German hymn of defiance, so that when they got to the last line they
were hardly able to distinguish between the Kingdom of God and the
Kingdom of Germany?

At the time when the persecution for the faith in the Church really
came upon us – as some people will still remember – we did not often
turn up this hymn. It was spoilt for us by false sentiment, and as the
persecution began to press upon us, we preferred to choose other
hymns from the time of the Reformation and newer ones which
described and expressed more credibly the situation of faith under the
assault of persecution. Thus as on the one hand we shun the sentiment,
the misuse and the misunderstanding, so on the other hand we shun the
sense of power that also expresses itself in this hymn of defiance, as it
does in the attitude of the Luther depicted in the Luther Monument at
Worms. That is not really the man of faith as we have learnt to see him
through our own time of trouble.

7

Is this hymn then to be suppressed, like other old patriotic songs of defiance from the Kaiser's day, which we mostly quote today only in irony? We could, I think, find a new relation to the hymn if we were thoughtfully to consider its content, and in so doing, were first to think what situation is being described by the people who sing "*A safe stronghold our God is still*". "*Our*" – we, a whole group is speaking there, not only an individual Christian who in solitude is struggling inwardly with his God. Such things do happen – but clearly this is not what is happening here, a group of people together are in the situation that is here being described. It is a frightful situation. It is not living in peace, it is not enjoying tolerance, it has no legal status. It is involved in a life and death struggle with enemies from whom it can expect no quarter. A campaign of annihilation is being waged against it, and that by a hostile power overpoweringly dominant, which has all the world's means of compulsion at its disposal. The "*Prince of ill*" who "*looks grim as e'er he will*", and there is on earth no ally who could change the situation "*on earth is not his fellow*". And lest anyone think that these are merely external pictures to describe inner conflicts of faith, it is clearly said that real, material, conflicts are under consideration. "*Goods, honour, child and wife*" – everything that makes life on earth worth living, can be snatched from them. And it will be snatched from them, for the world is "*all devils o'er, and watching to devour them*", and "*with force of arms we nothing can, full soon were we down-ridden*". That is their situation.

Why are they in this situation? Strangely enough, this hymn does not tell us. Are they criminals who have the power of society against them? Are they terrorists, who have challenged the whole world? Are they a minority of different descent and colour, and therefore mercilessly persecuted by the majority? There is only one hint from which it can be guessed why they are in that situation. They say that "*for us fights the proper man, whom God himself hath bidden*", and he is given the remarkable name, "*Jesus Christ, the Lord Sabaoth's Son*" then it says "*there is no other God*". There is no other God. This group says that in a world which is full of gods, in which gods appear everywhere, and claim from men sacrifice and obedience and honour. It denies all this, refuses to go along with it, and says "*there is no other God*". The ally who fights for them, seems to have required this of them. He is only their ally when they break with all other allies, with all other gods, and refuse them obedience. What they are suffering now is the punishment for their having been enticed to such action by their one ally. That has not made their life more peaceful and secure, but has let loose the destructive fury of the devils of the whole world upon them; that has changed the gods of this world into devils who oppose them. Where do we find such a group? Obviously not here among ourselves. The situation described here does not at all fit the Protestant and Catholic Church in our country. They are not deserted by all the world. They are publicly respected, protected by the State. It is, on the contrary, politically dangerous to attack the Church. What threatens it, at the most, is a great indifference, but not that vindictive enmity and destructive fury of the great and powerful of this world, to which the small group of this hymn is exposed. With us it brings no penalty to confess Jesus Christ, on the contrary, it is profitable, – e.g. in one's official career and in many other cases. Where does it bring a penalty?

We think first of all of the Christians in Communist lands. True, there the time of the worst persecutions is over. It was in Russia the same as it was at the beginnings of the Lutheran movement. It could lead to imprisonment and the stake when a man said *"There is no other God"*. Today in the east, thank God, the persecution has slackened, but all the same, a man who confesses Christ and does not worship the god Party, and submit himself with his conscience to it unconditionally, has to pay for it with his family and in his profession by all sorts of disadvantages, and every now and then, individuals, like some Baptists in Russia, have to suffer far more, or they break into revolt, and fall into despair, like our brother Oscar Brüsewitz, who committed suicide by setting himself on fire.

Even there in Russia, it is not really faith itself as such that comes in conflict with authority, but behaviour that results from faith. If there a state-philosophy is mandatory, the reason is that the authorities wish to direct action by means of controlling thought. For this reason Christians come into conflict with authority in that country, because in their behaviour they confess that *"There is no other God"*. With us in the west a tolerant pluralism is the rule. You can believe in one God, or in ten gods, or in none; it makes no difference at all, that does not worry anybody. Thus the description of the situation does not seem to apply to us, because the confession *"There is no other God"* has for me and you no disadvantageous results. Thus it seems that we certainly can't here sing *"A safe stronghold our God is still"*.

But if we look back over the frontiers of our Church Idyll in the Federal Republic, then things are different. In Latin America priests and laymen go to the unfortunate masses in the slums, and set up there medical centres, and schools for illiterates, and help them to organize themselves and help the families of prisoners, and support the striking workers – and already they are disturbing the interests of the powerful – the gods in these lands, because by their actions and not only by their words they are confessing Jesus as their Lord, and already it looks for these men as if *"This world were all devils o'er"*. The German Father Lunkenbein, who lived many years among the Indians of the Amazon, was shot there a few weeks ago. Together with the Indians he disturbed the interests of big business – among them our Volkswagen Firm, and so we Germans have a big share in this. These big concerns are trying to deprive these Indios there of their last possible means of livelihood, and to bring to its conclusion in these years the great murder of the Indians, of which the white races are historically guilty, without anyone in the white world raising a finger in protest. A Brazilian Bishop the other day, who was standing up in a police station in defence of three women who had been subjected to torture, saw his closest cooperator shot in front of him, with the warning that next time it would be his turn. News of this kind streams from Latin America to me in my house, from this whole continent, which today in the interests of big capital is being transformed into a hell for numberless tortured, hungry and enslaved human beings. Or in South Korea; the other day a group of South Koreans came to me, every one of whom had a brother or relative who was a pastor or a church member who had already been crippled by violence or was awaiting imminent captivity. A Confessing Church has come into being there which is much harder put to it than we were in the times of the Confessing Church during our Church struggle, much more oppressed, tortured, maltreated, because they are standing up for human rights. If we go round the globe to South Africa, and wherever we may, the same thing holds good, Faith has for its consequences loving behaviour, if it is not content to be sheer chatter and egoism. And when faith in love goes outwards, and becomes a real way of life, then it will disturb powerful interests, and that even in our own country. Even in our case it can happen that an individual or a whole group, by its action according to the instructions of Christ, suffers loss in respect of family, rights, and profession, and that the prospect is so desperate that they also must say *"Full soon were we down-ridden"*. Imagine yourself in the position of such people in Paraguay, in Namibia, in South Korea, in Chile, in the Soviet Mental Hospitals – shall we then still sing *"A safe stronghold is still our God"*? Is it thinkable that in torture chambers there is anything but despair? So it is impossible for us here to sing the hymn, because we are not in that situation – and impossible to sing for those that are in that situation, because all singing dies on one's lips there, and perhaps also because all faith dies there? A miracle would have to happen, if a man and a group in such a situation can still say *"The city of God remaineth"* – that is, our membership of God's kingdom, our possession of true life, true happiness, even when our body is shattered and our earthly happiness destroyed. What enables men to grasp such a hope so that they can then have faith, and perhaps even in the torture chamber can sing, in the slime of imprisonment and the slums, a thing that has repeatedly happened in the years of our century, which is rich as few others have been in the witness given by Christian living and dying? Hope can arise in those who have already lost it when they hear one of their tortured cell companions who has groaned with them, whispering "My God, my God, why hast Thou forsaken me?", and who now whispers to them, "It's true, all the same. We have done the right thing to take the road we have. We must not regret it, we are not lost. He does not forsake his cause or his people, *'He shall conquer in the battle'*." The same confederate who drew them into this way which now causes such bitter loss in goods, honour, children and wife, and in their own bodies, Jesus Christ himself, lies tortured beside them, and has at the same time as the risen one broken through all defeats to victory. Through him there speaks to them the God of whom they have said

"There is no other God", saying *"I am with you with my Spirit and my gifts, I am your safe stronghold, your trusty shield and weapon.* And you will yet see that you have not to regret your failure to respect the gods. They are not gods, they are only destroyers, and they are only powerful so long as people fear them. And because the whole world fears them, that is the reason why the world is in such a dreadful condition. And you, who have broken with them, you will see, you are not on the losing side, but on the victorious side."

I say it, and repeat it, hope can arise, and the miracle that I am describing here has happened time and again in this century of ours, and happens everywhere that faith, which is active through love, comes in conflict with the great divine and demonic powers of this earth. When love does not come into conflict, then it can well happen because it is holding itself within limits inside of which it runs no risks, in which nothing happens to us, and everyone merely claps in approval, because it is always an edifying spectacle for other people when a few loving people are there. But when love does not respect such boundaries, then it comes into conflict. And from this we may learn that faith leads us into the way of love, but love that presses on determinedly forward comes into such deadly conflicts in this world that it must again take refuge in faith.

These Christians of whom we can hear much today, in the prisons of South America, Chile, South Korea, and so on, are not there alone. They lie there tortured and mishandled and deprived of freedom and life, in the midst of others who by necessity and rebellion or from humanity and a feeling for justice have likewise come into conflict, risking themselves to help the need of their fellow-men – have come into conflict with the great powers who are today transforming the earth into a common grave for untold hungry and persecuted and deprived people.

What have Christians to distinguish them from their comrades in conflict and suffering? They hear, where no earthly ally can help them, an ally speaking to them, in their utter forsakenness they find they are not forsaken. Their ally suffers with them, and at the same time has gone before them to victory. By this he gives them inward confirmation that the way into which he has brought them is the right way, which they must not regret having taken, even if they have to pay with *"goods, honour, children, wife"* – or as has happened to many women in these lands and prisons, with child and husband, with all that is dear and precious to them in the world. He encourages and strengthens them by *"his Spirit and his gifts"*, he asks them to look forward to victory, and gives them assurance that God has not handed over this world to the devils, but will rescue them out of their hand, and that they are not suffering for a lost cause, but for the triumphant cause – *"Not they can overpower us"*. Ever and again the miracle happens, that people who had every reason for fear and were overwhelmed by fear, by reason of this word begin to say *"We lay it not to heart so sore"*, and their fearlessness irradiates their comrades in the struggle and suffering, and strengthens the dispirited, so that they do not give up, do not become traitors, do not go over to the enemy, do not sink to death in despair.

All this seems far away to us. We are not in South Korea, or in Latin America or in the Soviet Union, or even in East Germany. We have such a comfortable life as Christians, and when we confess our faith, the world is not transformed into a world full of devils. But that situation can come near to us, firstly, when we take part in the struggles of our brothers in distant lands, as we undertake to do in the one Christian Church, the communion of saints. We can only take part when we are informed and do not hold this depressing information at arm's length. And, having this information, we are led to intercession and supportive action. Then their situation touches us closely. Secondly, these experiences of powerlessness and this fear will not remain wholly strange to us. This will happen at that moment when in our case too, faith becomes active in love, and our love does not cautiously confine itself within limits which do not conflict with powerful interests. And, thirdly, a question. It might be the case that we live so comfortably, because our understanding of Christianity is such that it only holds good for our inner life, and creates no difficulties in outward behaviour. We say *"There is no other God"*, but cunningly and busily we worship other divine powers of this world beside the one God in order to protect *"Goods, honour, children, wife"*. That is the question which the fate and the struggle of the Christian communities today over a large part of the world poses to our Christian Church here, and to each one of us. As participants by intercession in this struggle we shall now be able to sing, perhaps as the expression of a new hope, a trembling hope, one that needs, and receives consolation. Quietly, reflectively, no longer with enthusiasm but in an undertone let us sing together:

> A safe stronghold our God is still,
> A trusty shield and weapon,
> He'll help us clear from all the ill
> That hath us now o'ertaken.

Lord our God, we have ourselves been privileged to experience, and others testify to us, that your Word is able to confront all unhappiness and all persecution, that your Word can conquer our despair, drive out our fear, can create and strengthen new faith. Therefore we thank you for your Word and ask you, "Make us your servants, to spread it everywhere".

We pray you for those whom we have named, those whom we have not named, and those of whom we know nothing, although we ought to know about them, and those about whom we can know nothing, all whom your way of obedience has led into suffering, together with their comrades in suffering we commit into your hand, and pray for your Spirit and your gifts for them, that they may be able to shine forth upon all despairing people around them, and to strengthen their comrades in suffering, so that no one gives up, betrays or despairs. We pray for all peacemakers in Southern Africa, in Lebanon, in North Ireland, and all who help to ensure that the way of violence and oppression is forsaken. Today, on this day when we remember the Reformation, and the division which came into being in Christendom through the freedom of your Word, we bring before you also the shame and the weakness of these divisions among Christians, and pray you to help us to seek unity with the brothers in the other denominations of Christendom, in order to serve together the need of the world. Bless and protect and guide the work in the World Council of Churches, we lay on your heart, Lord, our Church in West Berlin, and its Bishop, all who preach in it, and who give service of many kinds, at the organ, in the hospitals, all the Church workers and helpers. Make us a congregation of your free Word, men who are active in love, and confess that you alone are the God whom we must fear and love. Help us to believe and to love.

The Consequences of the Hymn of Praise

Long ago you began to win back your lost world for yourself. You have
even reached us, and made us members of your Kingdom, but our eyes
are so blind to your victories. We see only the victories of the powers
that do not wish to let you come to rule, the power of money, the power
of arms, and the power of folly, and the power of all the difficulties in
which we have entangled ourselves. It deceives us, makes us cowards,
makes us doubt in your power, and doubt that we shall reach the goal.
We pray you, forgive us, that we are such poor witnesses
to your Kingdom. May your Kingdom triumph in us and the world,
and make us servants of your Kingdom, tomorrow better than we
were yesterday. Lord, have mercy upon us!

I have asked some friends what I should preach about in the five
services for which I am responsible in this winter term. One of them
said to me! "You never preach on the Psalms, preach on the Psalms."
Now I have not chosen special texts for this purpose, but I would like
this winter to speak about the individual parts of the 118th Psalm.

*O give thanks unto the Lord, for he is good; his steadfast love endures
for ever! Let Israel say "His steadfast love endures for ever". Let those
who fear the Lord say "His steadfast love endures for ever". Let those
who fear the Lord say, "His steadfast love endures for ever".*
Psalm 118, 1–4.

"After they had sung the hymn of praise, they went out to the Mount of
Olives." Thus the Evangelist Matthew begins his account of the arrest
of Jesus in Gethsemane (26, 30). The hymn of praise, the "Great
Hallel", which was sung in Israel at the Passover meal, consisted of
Psalms 113–118. At the beginning of the meal Psalms 113 and 114
were sung, and Psalms 115–118 at the end of this meal. So now also did
Jesus, the Jew from Nazareth, with his disciples at his last Passover
meal, in which we join at every Lord's Supper as also invited guests,
and as people also privileged to be present. From the singing of this
hymn then Jesus sets out on his way towards Gethsemane and Golgotha. This is the way Jesus took, these are the consequences he drew
from the hymn of praise, that is his way of putting the hymn of praise
into practice, to go of his own free will to Gethsemane and Golgotha.
To follow Jesus means to follow him on this way, to be ready to do this,
and only if we follow Jesus have we really the right to sing his hymn of
praise. When, thirty years ago, we came into some persecution, this
Psalm came near to us, and we came near to this Psalm. I remember a
great Intercessory Service in 1938 in the central church in Jena, during
a wave of imprisonments. I read this Psalm 118, and the congregation
took up the words, and spoke them along with me and they were most
genuinely our words, and at the same time words that had been put in

our mouths, which lifted us above ourselves, and created more freedom in us than we ourselves had possessed, freedom to go the way of discipleship, even to imprisonment, to the concentration camp, to death.

This way, with its final consequence, was at that time required of only a few of us, and at that time we reflected too little that the same words, at the same time, the words of this Psalm of praise, were not sung only by us, not only in German, but in Hebrew, by Jewish families at the Passover meal, in much greater affliction, defamed and dishonoured, slandered and robbed and left in the lurch by all their neighbours, even their Christian neighbours, with the prospect of murder ever more clearly before their eyes. Thus they sang, and fortified themselves by this song of praise for the road to death, as Jesus fortified himself with the song of praise on his way to death. And, however contradictory this may seem, the hymn of praise and the way to death, that is the mystery of the Gospel. The purpose of the whole of the Gospel is to fortify us with hymns of praise for our way to death, as each one of us has to tread it, in order that the way to death may become a way of life.

When Jesus with this hymn of praise upon his lips sets out for Gethsemane and Golgotha, then the first thing that this has to say to us is, that such a hymn of praise, such thanks for God's goodness, is not limited to cheerful hours, and not the fruit of cheerful hours. We have profoundly misunderstood what the Bible says about the love of God, if we think that this is an idea which came to men in a satisfying situation, where they are merely expressing in religious concepts the sentiment "Life is beautiful, and we have it good". An idea that is valid for the sunny days of existence, but which disappears when the leaf turns, when, like Job, we sit in misery and ashes, when we writhe in the spasms of cancer, and when we are dragged to the torture chamber. In reality, we hear the men of faith speak more of the love of God, *"He is good, his steadfast love endureth for ever"* more in days of affliction than in good days. Jesus is the example of this, he went with open eyes to death with the hymn of praise on his lips. We hear them speak of God's love and recognize this love, they call out from the Cross, and from situations under the Cross, from that very place with trembling and then ever stronger voice saying *"Give thanks unto the Lord, for he is kind, and his steadfast love endureth for ever"*.

With this, Jesus says on the way to the Cross: that is how things will turn out; that will be the end result. Everything that is being done to you now, everything that will force from you the cry of dereliction, will not refute this, will not hinder this from being the eventual result. *"Thy steadfast love endureth for ever."* That is what the theologians call an eschatological confession, that is, a confession of hope with regard to the final outcome, a confession defying the present in the name of a still concealed future, the future of promise, that is laid hold of here and now. The night will not last for ever. It will not remain dark, the days of which we say that they give us no pleasure, will not be the last days. We

look forward through them to a light to which we now belong, and that
will not forsake us. That is our confession. When we now sing the hymn
of praise, then we anticipate, in the same words, the hymn of praise
which with seeing eyes we shall sing in eternity *"He is kind, his steadfast
love endureth for ever"*.

The word that is here translated by "steadfast love" – the Hebrew
word *chesed* is translated by Luther and the most of the German
versions of the Bible on the many occasions when it appears, by
"grace". The beautiful word "grace", which originally means "to turn
oneself to someone to help", even this beautiful word is unfortunately
so hackneyed, that some years ago a Jewish scholar proposed to clarify
it and make it come alive for us by using the modern word "solidarity".
The man who is solidary with us, who is consistently and wholly on our
side, shares everything with us, does not wish to be better off than us,
puts at stake for us everything that he has and can, fights for us, and will
see to it that we are saved. Now perhaps we value, or can guess at least
the immeasurable scope and the immeasurable daring of this hymn of
praise, which makes the Biblical message stand quite alone in the
world of religions and philosophies and world-views, because apart
from this biblical message no one has dared, with certainty, staking his
all upon it, to say "God is solidary with us". We are surrounded, not by
cold and empty nothingness, we are not ruled by blind fate, we are not
delivered into the hands of the torturers of this world, and we are not
awaited by the last executioner, death. We are surrounded, carried,
ruled and expected by an eternal Solidarity that stands on our side,
suffers with us, fights for us, sacrifices itself for us, and wins the future
for us. That is our reality, this is the source of our life. This Solidarity
gives us guidance for our life, and at the same time promises to stand in
for us when, through following its guidance, as is to be expected, we
meet hostility and the gravest affliction. This is the confidence of those
who hear and receive this Solidarity. Through this we ourselves
become solidary, for God is solidary with every one of his creatures,
with every other human being, even, – and about this much could be
said – with every animal. And when we treat in an opposite manner the
man who at our side is downtrodden and oppressed and hungry, and
ourselves tread others down and oppress them, then we are unsolidary
with the God who is solidary with this fellow-man, and whose solidarity
is the source of our own life.

Now it is clear that such an eschatological confession is not merely
some kind of prophecy for some future or other, but is a life-giving
confession which gives us an entry into this present world.

To believe means: now, today, against everything that denies it, to
hold with confidence that *"He is kind, and his steadfast love endureth
for ever"*; *To believe* means: to hear this Solidarity speaking with us,
and to speak with it, and to rely more on it than on all other solidarities,
with a reason for confidence which remains when all other reasons for
confidence collapse. *To believe* means to say "His steadfast love
endureth for ever" in the face of the bitterest loss, when we weep

beside a grave. And *to believe* means to be solidary with those with whom God is solidary, a messenger of the solidarity of God in relation to the man next to us, because he is not solidary with us without being solidary with the man next to us, Solidarity is freedom for the other man, as God is free for us.

This is the freedom of Jesus, with this hymn of praise he goes for us on the way to Gethsemane. And this freedom he imparts to his disciples. This freedom he proclaims in this hymn of praise to his people Israel; *"Let Israel now say, his steadfast love endureth for ever".* Without knowing him, they have heard his voice, when, through the centuries, oppressed by the unchristian Christians, they sang this hymn of praise at the Passover meals, and let themselves be strengthened by it for their way to death, and in their faithfulness to the fact that they are Jews, Israel, God's Israel. This hymn of praise they need again today, when in their land they live, a small company of two millions, threatened by death, surrounded by ever more deadly hostility, threatened by the prodigious arms of the oil multi-millionaires, abandoned by the most of the other states, and even yet without decisive solidarity on the part of Ecumenical Christianity, which it is high time for them to receive.

Israel was the first recipient and acknowledger and witness of the solidarity of God with his human race, that is destroying itself by its lack of solidarity. It became this recipient and acknowledger and witness, not for its own sake, but for the sake of all men. When Jews and Gentiles together struck down and hanged the King of Israel, in whom the Lord of Israel took the final step of solidarity, the doors were opened for us among the Gentiles to say together with Israel the hymn of praise, and for this reason it is written, *"Let them now that fear the Lord say that his steadfast love endureth for ever".* That includes us all. For as bearers of the Gospel of the love of God that drives out fear, there remains only one new fear, the fear of ceasing to sing the song of praise, and falling into the dumbness of despair, of fear, of hopelessness. And from this fear we must flee to God with the request to receive us back continually, to sing the hymn of praise which is given to our hearts and mouths, and thereby to prepare ourselves for every way of death, in order that every way of death may become a way of life.

For this we pray to you, our Lord, with all our songs of praise, which we say after you, and for which we thank you.

The Calling to a Brotherly Life

O give thanks unto the Lord, for he is kind, and his mercy endureth for ever. Our heavenly Father, through your kindness you wish to make us kind, through your brotherliness to transform us into brothers. But we stand in your way, and we stand in our own way. We are unwilling to relinquish our unbrotherliness, we do not trust ourselves to relinquish it, we consciously hold on to what is our own, and we are unwilling to give it away.

Therefore we are bad participants in the work of your brotherliness. We ask you, forgive us, continue to work upon us by your Spirit, that today and tomorrow we may serve you better than yesterday.

Out of my distress I called on the Lord; the Lord answered me and set me free. With the Lord on my side I do not fear. What can man do to me? The Lord is on my side to help me, I shall look with triumph on those who hate me. It is better to take refuge in the Lord than to put confidence in man. It is better to take refuge in the Lord than to put confidence in princes. All nations surrounded me; in the name of the Lord I cut them off! They surrounded me like bees, they blazed like a fire of thorns; in the name of the Lord I cut them off! Psalm 118, 5–12.

June 1530. Reichstag in Augsburg. The Reformation movement has made tremendous advances since the Reichstag at Worms, but has also suffered severe reverses. Powerful groups are working to have the Protestants declared heretical, falling under the condemnation of heresy, and that, according to the mediaeval practice in the case of heresy, which is still in operation, means extermination. The Emperor will then make a crusade against the Protestant princes and cities, which are in a minority, and, as it seems, there will not be a long future for them. In Augsburg itself the men of Wittenberg are represented by Melanchthon, that sensitive and apprehensive man. Luther himself, who cannot go thither because of the Imperial ban upon him, has betaken himself to the fortress of Coburg, which is the nearest place possible. From there he reinforces Melanchthon with splendid letters, and there he sets on paper one of his most beautiful writings, an exposition of the 118th Psalm, "The song beloved of the saints" as he calls it. Soon this work will be widely distributed under the title of "The Beautiful Confitemini", (because the first word of this Psalm in the Latin Bible is "Confitemini" "Confess the goodness of the Lord"), and it has since then comforted numberless people in deep distress. Luther himself, in his Introduction says that this Psalm "must be called mine, and be mine, since it has also deserved right well of me, and helped me out of many great distresses, where neither Kings nor Emperors, wise men nor saints could have helped me, and it is dearer to me than the riches and power and honour of the Pope, the Turks, the Emperor and all the world. So I would be unwilling to give this Psalm in exchange for all of them".

Since in the last week we have been thinking with gratitude of the Reformation, it is very fitting that we should look more closely at this Psalm which was so important for Luther. Luther, that central figure of the Reformation movement, – in spite of all the criticism which is made of him today – with which I feel in sympathy on many individual points of his behaviour and his theology – remains one of the greatest witnesses of faith of the Church, and so rich and original and gracious an expositor of the Bible as has seldom been given to the Church. He loved such songs of victory as this Psalm. That he composed several Easter hymns, but never a Good Friday hymn, is characteristic of him. It is from this that the idea of him has arisen, as a strong unyielding man, such as the famous Luther monument in Worms represents him; a powerful man with the Bible before his breast, looking straight forward, "And were the world all devils o'er", nothing can overthrow him.

The popular picture of Luther is however a very superficial picture of him, the picture of a man immune to temptation. In that case we envy him and admire him, but that means that he is very far removed from us much-tempted men. In reality Luther was a man in whose experience and life and thought and theology temptation had a central place. It is true that he once said that when for the first time he read the polemic of a papal theologian against him, he was at first afraid. "Then I thought, should it happen that the tipsy madman writes such things about me, then our God gave me grace and I had to laugh. Since then I have never been frightened!" An astonishing word "Since then I have never been frightened!" And just that would remove him far from us, who are so much frightened. But again, it must be said, in reality he was, and increasingly in his old age, a man deeply tempted, very anxious, terribly divided. "From the wilderness, 1st July 1530", that is how he heads the Introduction to his "Beautiful Confitemini". "From the wilderness" – that brings him near to us, for the wilderness, the parched lands, the lands of thirst, of dryness of faith, in which no fresh flowers bloom, where everything withers, and we can no more hope that something will come to flower and fruit, these times are not unknown to us. Luther's faith, words of the faith that are assured of victory, have come out of the wilderness and have been kept alive in the wilderness. To believe means for him to speak already in anticipation of victory in the midst of the wilderness, and to look forward to victory, not to despair of victory.

Here indeed, in this Psalm, there stands a real victor, and gives his cry of victory. He has the battle behind him; he breathes again, and lets his sword sink, takes off his helmet, wipes away the sweat and blood, and gives vent to his satisfaction, – "They surrounded me like bees, but in the name of the Lord I have destroyed them". That is indeed fine, splendid when a man again has the battle behind him. When he has come through, the demons have withdrawn, and one can laugh in retrospect. And the first thing is, not to forget that this can happen, time and again, that we have the battle behind us, that we are through, that we shall come through and come out of it.

But this victor wishes to be, not far away, but near to all who have not yet got so far, who are still in the wilderness, and are tiring themselves out in the struggle, and look to him enviously. Therefore he speaks, not only of victory, but of how it was previously, and says to everyone who is still trapped in the pit and the wilderness and the struggle; "I was just in the same situation as you! The water rose to my neck. In fear I was hopelessly trapped in it. The Hebrew word for "anguish", like the German word *"Angst"* is connected with the word *"eng"* (narrow) when a man feels constriction in his breast, and his lungs choke, and he has no more air and power to breathe; when they come at me from all sides, and I can't get my head above it. I am boxed in. Everything goes wrong with me. A hopeless disproportion between the powers on the other side that oppose me, and my own feebleness. *"They surround me like bees."*

"All nations", he says, all the Gentile nations, says Israel, all the Gentile nations surround me with deadly enmity, and do not give me a chance, not then, and not thirty years ago, and today again not. And in the midst of Israel Jesus, after he had sung this hymn of praise, this Psalm, crossing over to the Mount of Olives, to Gethsemane, sang, "What can man do unto me?" Was it frivolity, was it illusion? O, what men can do to him and to us all! In Jerusalem we can still see today in the house of Caiaphas the two pillars in the cellar to which they bound him, his hands and his feet, and lashed him with whips into which pieces of metal were inserted, which tore out the flesh. And then they dragged him out and nailed him up there, and caused him to die one of the most fearful deaths that the sadistic spirit of man ever invented. That is what men can do to him. Man is man's worst enemy. What nature can do to us by illness or catastrophe is far outstripped by what men can do to one another. The mercilessness and cruelty of men outstrips the indifference of nature. Often in those days when Jesus' Jewish brothers were murdered, we have prayed together with frightened people the words of David, "I am in a great strait; let us fall now into the hand of the Lord, for his mercies are great, and let me not fall into the hand of man (2 Sam. 24, 14). And Jesus says here, "What can man do unto me?"

It is not frivolity, it is no illusion. No, it is with seeing eyes that he goes forward to meet what men can do to him. And why? Here there is a task, a mission, a great cause, and behind the task there is one who commissions him, and the task, the mission, and the great cause are dear to him, and the one who commissions him is dear to him, and without him and his cause he would not wish to live. And so he sings to the one who sent him the hymn of praise, *"He is on my side, I will not fear"*, and goes straight forward into the trap, the despair, the unbelief, towards all the enemies that choke the breath out of him, into the midst of the forsakenness where he is abandoned by the one who promised not to abandon him, "My God, my God, why hast thou forsaken me?"

What is this mission that makes him ready to let himself be sent thus into that which men can do to him? What is the mission of Jesus? To make men human, to make inhuman men human, brotherly, for the sake of God's brotherliness, because inhumanity and unbrotherliness is destroying all of us. Into this mission to which Jesus obediently submits himself, into it he draws his disciples, and the transformation penetrates deep into the innermost motives of our spirits and our hearts. For unbrotherliness is deep-seated in us, as it is also in our conditions, and in the regulations of our society, in a world economic system, of which the World Council of Churches has just declared that its injustice is obvious, since it condemns millions of men to die of hunger, by maintaining an inequality by means of which we have enough and more than enough, and the others have too little to live. When Jesus attacks that with his disciples, this unbrotherliness that is so deep-seated in us and our condition, then he will meet with deadly enmity, then in east and west the hunt will be up against those who act in this manner. Therefore men can do much to such people. How should such weak and timid and easily terrified people as us, who so love their own lives, become human people, set free for brotherliness, how should they hold fast to this mission of Jesus, in which they have been given a share, even when it costs them their lives? How should such faithless people become believing people, who hear of succour, and on the strength of it remain true?

The song of victory speaks also of this. It names the weapon with which this Victor has fought in his hopeless situation. He calls out to all others who are in the selfsame situation, recommending the use of this weapon. *"In the name of the Lord I have destroyed them."* "In the name of the Lord", that contains three directions for all fighters, and most explicitly for the struggles that lead to discipleship, the mission of Jesus, the command of God's brotherliness to lead the brotherly life, but then, and from that point for all wildernesses into which we come, for all battles in which we are involved through personal difficulties, in troubles connected with money, and anxieties about illness and old age, and what ever else can be thought of. The first; make your calculations right as you look forward! We know that; daily we look ahead to tomorrow and the day after; how things will turn out, and we continually estimate in so doing our powers, our health, our vitality, our cunning, our money that we have at our disposal, our insurances, our shares, our allies, and the more we look ahead and calculate, we know that the greater become our anxieties, the greater the powers that oppose us, the more dangerous that which man can do to us, the smaller the chances that we shall still come through, the smaller our own resources, and the more our heart sinks, and the more we are inclined to give up. *"In the name of the Lord I have destroyed them"*; that is; take into account first of all the decisive factor for disciples who are on a mission, and this factor is himself, who sends us. His power is the greater power. "The floods of the sea have lifted up their voice and roar mightily, but the Lord is mightier" (Psalm 93, 3). *"It is better to trust in the Lord than to put confidence in men."* "It is good to put trust in God and not to put trust in princes" – in the powerful, in powerful allies, in powerful resources. Why? Are we not to make any use at all of these? Is that not also something good? Luther says very finely in commenting on the passage. "To rely and to use are two different things. God alone is to be trusted, creatures are to be used." So we should use the creatures and creaturely means of help, but, and that is the first direction – take into account the decisive factor, his promised support, and trust in him alone.

The second direction. It is only in the struggle that we have the experience, only in the struggle does certainty come, not before. It is not as if you had first of all your tremendous assurance of faith, which fills you, and then you think, now you can risk this struggle for the sake of God's cause, for the sake of brotherliness, which faces you now at this moment. That is not how it is. There is no guarantee beforehand. *He* gives no guarantee beforehand. Armed only with his name, not armed with feelings of faith and power, armed only with his name, he sends me into the struggle, lets me go into the wilderness, equipped perhaps still (and that is certainly important) by certain experiences of the past which I have had of his name, (and which others have had), with them I may go into the wilderness. Only in the struggle do our powers grow, only in the struggle is experience created, only in the wilderness is certainty of his presence created.

And the third direction; the weapon is his name. When Israel spoke of the name of the Lord, then it did not mean any name, like Jack or Fred or even Wotan or Jupiter, but the name that Moses heard calling out of the Burning Bush, the name that is given with four letters JHWH, we pronounce it today Jehovah or Jahweh. The Jews did better, and never spoke it out, but substituted another word, the word "The Lord" for it. These four letters have a meaning that was given to Moses in the story of the Burning Bush, (Ex. 3, 14). They have the meaning, "I am there, I will be there". That is the name of the Lord, and with this name Jesus crosses into Gethsemane and Golgotha. To hear this name, and while it seems as if he who has said "I will be there" were not there, to call in faith on him, and to trust him that in spite of all he is there. This name is the weapon of his people, to call on his name, to lay hold on this name, to defend ourselves in his name, in this name to attack everything that tries to deflect us from the mission of Jesus, from the mission of brotherly living, in the name of the God of brotherliness, whose name always contains two things, the task and the promise of aid. You must be brotherly, make the venture of brotherliness, and I shall be there, the living God, as your loyal brother. That then will happen, that we have experiences of fear and affliction, we shall be led into tribulation, *"They gather around me like bees"*. Then the other thing will also happen, that we defend ourselves with this name and win through, have experiences of victory, and at the last, finally, and for ever say "*I called in my distress unto him, 'the one who will be there', and he 'the one who will be there', set my feet in a large place*".

Therefore we pray to you, we who have heard this, to bring your name unforgettably into our hearts! Through it make us loyal to your mission, and give us experiences of victory, here in time, and there in eternity!

We think, Lord, today when we have heard your promises and challenges, and the songs of victory of your Son and your Church – we think today above all of those who see themselves far away from any victory, who are near the point of giving up the struggle, the struggle for life, the struggle for faith, the struggle for love, the struggle for a good cause. We think of all those who lie in the pit and see no light, on sick beds, in dryness of soul, all sorts of people in despair. We think, in your presence, of all those to whom the word of our witness is distorted through our bad witness and our false life, and to whom your word is only a sound, that merely reaches their ears, but not their heart. For all of them, among whom we also are sometimes included, we call to you, and ask you, as you have promised, take pity on them, let those who are in darkness see your light!

We pray to you also for the Synod of the Evangelical Church in Germany, which begins today in St. John's College, and also for the Synod of our Evangelical Church of West Berlin, which will begin next Sunday in St. John's College. We ask you, Lord, for the consultations of those whom we have sent as delegates, that they may take counsel together for the concerns of the whole Church, its difficulties, its reforms, its task, its improvements. We ask you for these deliberations, for illumination and empowering and resolve through your Spirit.

Lord, we are anxious about Israel in the midst of its enemies who surround it. Do not reckon against it the mistakes it has made! Change the hearts of the enemies. Give the Government of Israel wisdom and resolve to make decisions for peace. Let them all see together how necessary it is for them to live in peace with one another. Save, Lord, and protect your people Israel from new murders!

We pray to you for all who in this hour pray to you in their distresses and tasks, and we ourselves call to you, Lord, make the promise in your name come true! You are the one who will be there for us now and for ever.

Help for Living with Problems

Our Lord and Father,
when we wait upon you, we do not wait in vain. No one who waits on you, waits in vain. But we mostly expect too much from ourselves, and too little from you; that is why we so often end up with inexpectancy and hopelessness and despair, and so little power of hope comes from us. Forgive us, that we expect so little from you. Help us to become people who wait upon you, and to draw others into the hope of waiting upon you. Lord, have mercy upon us!

Hark, glad songs of victory in the tents of the righteous; "The right hand of the Lord does valiantly, the right hand of the Lord is exalted, the right hand of the Lord does valiantly." I shall not die, but I shall live, and recount the deeds of the Lord! The Lord has chastened me sorely, but he has not given me over to death. Psalm 118, 15–18.

Then, in 1530, when Martin Luther, as I told you last time, followed in painful suspense and anxiety in the Castle of Coburg the development of things at the Augsburg Reichstag, this Psalm 118 became so dear to him. On the wall of his living-room in the Castle of Coburg, he painted in bold letters the 17th verse, "Non moriar, sed vivam, et narrabo opera Domini", *"I shall not die, but live, and declare the works of the Lord"*.

When the Reichstag was over, and he could breathe again, and realize in relief that his friends in Augsburg had witnessed a good confession before the Emperor and the Empire, he asked a composer whom he valued highly, the then famous composer of motets, Ludwig Senfl in Munich, to set for him to music this seventeenth verse, and the "Non moriar" then often echoed in Luther's house and in the houses of his friends; "I shall not die, but live, and proclaim the works of the Lord". To live and to proclaim the works of the Lord means practically the same thing. And to proclaim the works of the Lord, that is to live!

What is meant by that? We have all had experience of people, who have got on our nerves because without a pause they tell us only of themselves and their works, and their song of triumph was always merely a song of self-praise. In this song of triumph here, the eyes of those who sing are drawn away from their own works to the works of one who is wholly other, and what they themselves have endeavoured and achieved sinks in wonder and admiration before what this ally has endeavoured and achieved. This turning away of our eyes from ourselves, and turning them to another is itself a part of the liberation in which this Psalm rejoices. For indeed that is an important and necessary liberation, to come out of this fixation of my eyes upon myself, my achievements and problems, my successes, and this merry-go-round circling around my own fame, to become free to look without jealousy and with appreciative eyes on the works of other people around us, thankful for their achievements and successes.

How this liberation comes about can be seen from this song of triumph. When he utters his cry of triumph, "They surrounded me like bees, but in the name of the Lord I have destroyed them, yes, in the name of the Lord I have destroyed them", that is not boasting of his own achievement, of what he has brought to pass, but boasting about the mighty acts of his covenant comrade, his great ally, in whom he rejoices. "Everything that we achieve, you have given us", says the prophet Isaiah (26, 12). Now our successes are transformed from our achievements into gifts which we have received. Instead of becoming vain, we become thankful, because we are thankful for the success of our covenant comrade to whom we owe everything in our success. And in this our eyes are opened also to that which is given to others round about us. We can congratulate them on their success without jealousy, and we can be glad that others have successes – as a gift that through them is given also to us. We are freed from our own self-conceit, which is so great a nuisance among us men. All our power has been given us by you.

That is the language of faith, Faith is a good insight into things. When we hear the Gospel, and begin to believe in it, then we see through the surface, through the foreground of reality. On the surface, in the foreground is to be seen all that our eyes see, what our normal consciousness grasps, nature, things, men, the operation of nature and the operation of men. So long as we know nothing of faith, so long as we know nothing of God, the only thing that we see is this foreground, the operation of nature and the operation of men. But when we hear and believe, we see through the surface and the foreground the living God at work, his continued giving and helping. What happens in the foreground is shot through by his activity, that is a struggle between his activity and everything that works against him.

This new insight of faith, which through the foreground sees the living God at work, is an incredible liberation, not only from vanity, but also from fear. So long as we do, as most people do, and as we too who are hearers of the Gospel do through long periods of our life, so long as we see merely the surface, the superficial reality, so long we must believe that we have to do everything ourselves. And that is necessarily a situation of great anxiety. Here we stand under a constant pressure to achieve. Here there confronts us the greatness of the tasks, which outstrip our powers, and it is no wonder that people become neurotic, because they continually have the feeling that they cannot make it. The power of the obstacles, both those without and those within us, confronts us. That is because of our poor equipment of faith and love. How then can all this be without great anxiety? To see through things, and to see the active, living God at work, who himself takes responsibility for events, and for his having set us weak inadequate people to work – that gives new confidence, then the new insight begins which contradicts the old anxiety. Then there are battles where anxiety is defeated by hope, and we can begin anew and look around us in freedom. "The Lord is with me, what can men do to us?"

But now there is the other thing, which is also included in our passage, the new vision of faith as a penetration through the foreground to the essential thing, God's reality. Reality means effectual power. To see God's effectual power behind the visible things and events in the world. This new insight of faith concerns not only our ability, and our activities, and the ability and activities of other people, but just as much our suffering. For that is in truth a good part of our reality, the reality of our life, what we have to bear with, because we are beings of this nature, and exposed to its assaults, and because we are members of society, and exposed to the assaults of other people – exposed also to the catastrophes of history – think only of the catastrophes of our century! What a lot of suffering is summed up there! But this is only increased when a man enters the discipleship of Jesus, cannot resist any longer the call of Jesus, but is drawn by him into new activity, into all the provocations that discipleship signifies for the environing world, and of which these weeks here in Berlin have given some evidence. What an outcry, when a Bishop dares to act in a Christian manner, as a Bishop ought to do! How both the world outside the Church, and the world inside the Church hurls itself upon him! And what calumnies, and what hard days these two young people, Undine Zühlke and Cornelius Burkhardt had to go through, in the prison cell, and persecuted by the Press as criminals and supporters of gangs of murderers!

Everyone that wanted to know, could know that from the start there was no suspicion of complicity in them, and that they had done nothing but try to protect the Synod of the Evangelical Church in Germany from certain disturbances. Now it can be that times are coming in which, looking back, we shall say that, however small, these were sufferings of disciples of Jesus Christ. But an indication of the fact that not only is suffering a part of being human, but that it belongs especially to discipleship, could be learnt by us from these weeks.

Now this Psalmist sees through the foreground of suffering and the infliction of suffering the God who stands behind, and works in all this in concealment. What he recognizes in this he expresses in very old-fashioned language, the language of an ancient pedagogy. "*The Lord hath chastened me sore.*" That is the language of the ancient pedagogy, which took it for granted that the rod was an essential instrument of true parental love. It is to be hoped that we have left all these pedagogical ideas behind us. But we shall have to think ourselves into the situation, when the witnesses of faith of earlier times bear witness to the Gospel in their own modes of thought and language. For them there was no contradiction between the rod and parental love; the two things belonged inseparably together. Now he says in the language of the old pedagogy: As it dawns on a child who has become reasonable, that the pains which his parents inflicted on him in punishment were not inflicted in anger but out of loving concern, seeking the best for him, wishing to instruct him, and warning him with the help of pain, in order that he may never forget – as this dawns upon a child who has become reasonable, so now I realize that after I had cried out with bitter reproaches against him, who had promised help and deserted me, "Why do you permit that, why do you make me suffer so cruelly, why do you yourself torture me so cruelly?" – it dawned on me through hearing your promise that even in suffering your love is active, you are taking trouble with me, you wish to impress on me something that otherwise I would not have learnt; your wish is to bring me to new experiences, even to new liberations. *"He has chastened me sorely, but he has not given me over to death."* We note it well, here we touch, here the Psalm itself touches on the difficult question about the meaning of suffering. It is not as if this Psalmist meant with his report *"He has chastened me sorely"*, that he had given an account of all the meaning of suffering. What we hear in the Gospel about the meaning of suffering is not a key to answer for us all questions about ourselves and concerning the lot of other men and the whole ocean of sufferings which fills the history of the world. The man who believes that the Gospel will answer all questions will always be bitterly disappointed. And the man who believes that the Gospel will unravel for us the meaning of suffering will also be disappointed. We must be glad if now and then – and that seems to have happened to the Psalmist – if now and then a little we can see a little bit of meaning in our sufferings, or the sufferings of others, recognize a little that perhaps there a just judgement is being passed, or that a purification is happening there, or that I have learnt more, and at the end say "I would not like to have been without these hard years in my life". That is a little bit of meaning – thank God, when we get it. But the real significance of the Gospel in the question about the meaning of suffering is, that it helps us to live with unsolved problems, where the answers are not yet given to all our questions of "Why?". In this time of questioning the living and active God suffers with us himself in his Son upon the Cross, and calls out with us "Why?", and promises us from the Cross that we shall get an answer which will bring peace to us. So that we trust to him for the answer that we do not yet have.

It is perhaps just in this that the significance of such a song of victory becomes clearer to us, in relation to the suffering in which we and the whole world are still so deeply entangled. It is the victory song of the community of the proven ones (as Martin Buber translates the phrase "community of the just"), the song that the community of the proven ones, the community of those who have won through, at the close, at the end of days, on the day of Jesus Christ, will sing in the Kingdom of God, on the day of the answer, when all our conflicts in all our sufferings will have come to peace. This victory song says that, now already, with human words of today, and challenges us now already, to join our voices to it. This "now already" – that means Advent. For Advent is the situation in which we have not yet reached fulfilment, in which we still stand before the gate, still in the dark valley where we require the rod and the staff, still are looking for the light, and are glad of every ray of light. In Advent, anticipating and looking forward to the fulfilment, some people, in an apparently quite untimely manner are already singing the song of victory. They sing so loud that they even say of the greatest enemy, of him whom the Apostle Paul calls the last enemy of God, that he no longer has any significance. For when here the song of victory calls *"I shall not die but live"*, then our view of the foreground of things will object to the singer that we all die. He says *"He has chastened me sorely, but he has not given me over to death"*. We are all given over to death, and many are the names of those who then and today from loyalty to God's cause and from loyalty to the cause of man have gone to torture and death.

Then what can this mean, *"I shall not die but live"*. At that time, in his exposition of Psalm 118, when nothing had as yet been won, when everywhere Protestant martyrs were still dying, Luther wrote "Does that not mean dead when you are burnt, beheaded, drowned, throttled, condemned, hunted out of existence?" Indeed that is a good interpreter when someone can make out of the word "death" a salutary rod. The art to do this must be taught by the Holy Spirit and the right hand of God. Here we really have need of a good expositor who can shout down and overcome the devil with this verse and say. "And yet it is not death or wrath, and yet I know that he will not hand me over to death even were all the devils in hell to say it with one voice, yes, even if an angel from heaven were to say it. He will not kill me; I feel death indeed, but will not feel it, and shall not call it death, but hold on to the gracious right hand of God. Such a man does not deny that God will send him such a death, but he has an agreement with God."

That is a great word, "an agreement with God". Time and again in the darkest hours of war and imprisonment, the words of the "Cherubinic Wanderer" Angelus Silesius, were helpful to me, "In all eternity/No sound can be so fair/as when the heart of man/Is kept in tune with God", if I can thus say "Yes". The hard question – often less in our own suffering than in the suffering of others, confronted by the dreadful power of evil opponents and evil powers, by the reverses of a cause that made a good beginning – the hard question is whether I can say "Yes" to the concealed activity of God when in the foreground in what my eyes see, things go so against God and his promises, and I see only the defeats of God and not the victories of God. But we shall stand in agreement with God at the end, in the day of Jesus Christ, at the consummation, and now already we say our "Yes" to God's concealed will and to his inscrutable purposes in the certainty that at the end we shall sing his praise.

But that already transforms everything here. In our tasks it gives us endurance to stand at our post and remain where Jesus has placed us. In successes it protects us from vanity, and gives us thankfulness and modesty. In our reverses it gives us toughness and stamina, not to give up in the face of enemies and slanderers, protects us from bitterness, and helps us to pray for them that they may be freed from their fetters of wickedness and prejudice, and anxiety and hate. In dangers it makes us hold up our heads, banishes fear, and helps us to laugh. In suffering it gives us patience to listen again to the consoling word of promise "I am near you. I shall also help you." In dying we can then put our life in his hands, and know that in his hand the cause is not lost, that it is never lost. A life not lost – that is our song of victory in eternity.

Thankfulness Makes Life Whole

You know well all the guilt that each one of us has incurred, more
exactly than each one of us knows it. You see that we, your people,
often bring more shame than honour to your name. All this has not
discouraged you from coming to us. Therefore we pray to you, do not
let yourself in the future be discouraged by all that is wrong in our lives!
Make us, unprofitable and unjust as we are, through your forgiveness
disciples whom you can use! Lord, take pity on us!

*Open to me the gates of righteousness, that I may enter through them and
give thanks to the Lord. This is the gate to him, the righteous shall enter
through it. I thank thee that thou hast answered me and hast become my
salvation. The stone which the builders rejected has become the chief
cornerstone. This is the Lord's doing; it is marvellous in our eyes.*
Psalm 118, 19–23.

A gate is a symbol for a dividing line, for an incision into a life. Before
the gate, within the gate, outside and inside, things look different.
When it is a prison, then outside there is freedom, and inside night and
fetters, and, when it is Brazil or Chile, the torture chamber. When it is
the other way round, as it is here, a *"gate of righteousness"* then outside
there is night and error, and inside, the fullness of life, an illuminated
life, lights, and joy. Men stand before the gate and knock and wish to
enter, that is the situation into which the Gospel brings us when it
enters into our life, and makes us men who knock. It brings us to the
gate leading to full, complete, true life, and makes us men who knock.
For it makes us demanding, shameless men, who are no longer content
with what men here call life, with this vegetative life that leads to the
grave, and this treadmill and rat-race for livelihood and reputation and
advancement, each for himself, and remaining in the swim and having
power over other people. What sort of a life is that? And it is not to be
wondered at, if everywhere children are turning their backs on their
parents' homes, where people have made do with this wretched vegetable life, and say straight out to their parents "This is no kind of life
that you are offering us and living yourselves; real life must look quite
different". Perhaps these children who are unsatisfied and are themselves in search of something else, and yet not setting up anything
better, have heard a whisper of the Gospel – namely that the Gospel
makes us discontented with what we call life, and does this by empowering us to make a claim to real, full, satisfying, just and joyful
living. And so we stand before the gate of righteousness and knock at
it; "Open to me the beautiful gate of righteousness, Lead me into
God's house!" Just as then the procession of pilgrims in Jerusalem
stood before the Temple Gate, sang this Psalm, and knocked with the
cry, *"Open to me the gate of righteousness, that I may enter through it!"*
Then there came from within the cry from the Levites guarding the

gate, "This is the gate to him! The righteous make their entry through it". That is the call which stops our urgent knocking, because in this call there are contained two critical questions.

The first question: "Do you also know whither the gate leads?" It does not lead simply into a Utopia, not simply to the fulfilment of your wishes, which are, perhaps, crazy and self-seeking, and not simply into a full life as you yourselves now understand it. *"This is the gate to him"*, to the living God, to the light of life, to the light in which there is no darkness, and which tolerates no darkness, to the light which shines through your whole life, and brings to light every dark and unwholesome place in it. The gate leads through to the Last Judgement, before which no one and nothing in our life remains concealed.

The second question: "Do you also know who alone is permitted to go in here?" *"Righteous men go in here."* Or, as Martin Buber is wont here and elsewhere to translate: proven men go in here, proven coworkers with God, proven disciples of Jesus. Traitors, deserters, deceivers, fifth-columnists, have no entry.

Note: it does not say "Only Jews go in here, no Gentiles". It does not say "Only Christians or Church members go in here, no Jews or atheists or heathens". But it says "Proven men go in here. The Good Samaritan goes in here, who was neither a Jew nor a Christian, but did an act of mercy". Those people go in here who have visited the least of God's brothers in prison and in sickness, and who have clothed and fed them in hunger. Those go in here who as disciples of Jesus have not failed to confess him, nor to serve him in love.

We have long since stopped knocking, and stand there dismayed, and ask, how often in our life have we not failed, and how often in our life we have failed and ask of the Church how often it has failed or not failed. "The Christian Church has failed completely in the question of Israel and the Jews", said Archbishop Raya, the Catholic Archbishop of North Palestine the other day, as he left his post there, and that is only one point among many where we and the world around us reckon the Church to have failed. These are not the points which a great part of the Press and many Berliners hold against Bishop Scharf and Undine Zühlke and Cornelius Burkhardt as points of failure. The case is exactly the reverse of what the Press thinks; that in the Church in which these three took thought and acted, no adequately decisive steps were taken. The Church has not been decisive enough in its refusal to ally itself with power and riches in these two thousand years and as Friedrich Wilhelm Marquardt very rightly said in the meeting in the Musical Academy on 6th September, 1979, it has not been decisive enough in making the unprivileged groups, the failures, the neglected, the disabled and the outcasts, the central group for its concern and action.

And yet we know that when we speak of the Church, or of the failure of the Church, then we can never merely point to other people, as if the Church were a few people and a few officials who are in control of the Church. We are all the Church, and the failure of the Church reflects the continual failure of all of us, inasmuch as we thrust other people to one side and make ourselves, our own ego, the centre of all our doing and thinking.

The gate is closed, and the answer which came from within "The righteous go in here" has excluded us. "There is none that does good, no, not one" (Psalm 14, 3). The whole Bible, and above all, the New Testament, is full of the news that when men stand before the gate of life, this is not the last thing, this exclusion of us in outer night. There within, whence this call came which made us despair, *"The righteous go in there"* – there within is an Interest that will stand together with us, the unrighteous. The living God in his Kingdom does not wish to live alone with his righteousness. He wishes to have unrighteous men there with him. The disciples of Jesus, after the crucifixion and resurrection of Jesus, read and sang this Psalm, – it is quoted in the New Testament – and heard here the prophetic proclamation of a new history of God, an answer to the rejection that we experience before the gate. For they read here also the word *"rejection"*, and they had just taken part in a terrible story of rejection. There was a man for whom the outcast groups had become the central groups, who could not live without turning to the excluded, the tax-gatherers, the prostitutes, those who had gone wrong, the poverty-stricken masses who lived in unrighteousness and godlessness and knew nothing of God's commandments – to all of them he called "Come unto me, all ye that labour and are heavy-laden!", and they all thronged to him. All those who were involved in any great task of building, had no use for him. The Romans had no use for him in building up their great empire. The leaders of the Jewish people had no use for him in their tricky and subtle politics balancing between the occupying power and the masses of the people. The righteous had no use for him in the cultivation of their self-seeking piety. They all rejected him, but *"The stone which the builders rejected, hath God made the head-stone of the corner"*, the foundation and coping-stone of this gate for the building of his new kingdom, or, to change the figure, *the righteous man* the one righteous man who can enter here. The disciples of Jesus, his first congregation after Easter, found themselves invited, as it were, to creep under the cloak of Jesus, and concealed and protected by his cloak, to get themselves smuggled into the Kingdom of God, into the kingdom of life.

> My hope is built on nothing less
> Than Jesus' blood and righteousness;
> On Christ the solid rock I stand,
> All other ground is sinking sand.

The whole of the New Testament is full of this marvel. This is in truth *"marvellous in our eyes"*.

We often argue as to whether the miracles in the Bible really happened or not. An unprofitable argument; for in comparison with the one miracle of which the Bible is full, all other miracles pale. This one miracle is, that we who deservedly were shut out, are those who are undeservedly admitted. That is the miracle. And all the Biblical miracle stories – whether in the individual cases they happened thus or not is beside the point – are exemplary stories and signs which point to the one great reversal; we who deservedly were shut out, are undeservedly admitted. *This is the Lord's doing*, we did not do it ourselves. He alone had the power and the right to transform this exclusion to admittance. With all our efforts we could not have opened the gate from outside. He did it. Jesus is the opening of the gate of God's Kingdom to the excluded, and from within comes to us his call "Come unto me, all who labour and are heavy laden, with your unrighteousness and your failures even more than with your external misery, I will give you refreshment. Knock, and it shall be opened unto you."

What remains for us to do when all our previous action has not been able to open the gate, and never could have opened it? When with our previous action – whether it was a little better or a little worse – we must have stood for ever excluded from the locked gate of real life? What remains for us to do? And what will fill our life when one day we stand before the last gate, and then are permitted under the shelter of the cloak of Jesus, the one righteous man, to go through it?

Answer: *"I will go in and thank the Lord."*

To give thanks, that is the one thing that remains to do. To give thanks for what? The way that the Psalm puts it is very remarkable. *"I thank you that you bowed me"* (or, as Luther rightly translates; that you have humbled me) *"and save me"*. A person is humbled when it is made clear to him how great the discrepancy is between his opinion of himself and what he really has to offer. We shall never be saved, that is, brought out of the false life into the true life without being deeply humbled, without facing the moment of truth. Martin Buber translates the word "Gate of righteousness" by "Gate of truth", the bitter, painful truth. The illusions which we cherish about ourselves, are shattered, the excuses with which we so carefully cosset ourselves, are swept away. Usually, when someone does that to us, takes from us our illusions about ourselves, we are not wont to be grateful to him, but turn our backs on him in anger. The great change which Jesus, when we meet him, works in us, is that we are grateful to him that he tells us the truth about ourselves, and leads us into the truth, even the bitter and painful truth which ends all illusions. He holds the mirror of truth before us, in which we see our true selves. And see what happens then! When we are with him we do not run away from ourselves, and put up new excuses; together with him we face up to the truth, the end of illusion.

That is one part of our gratitude. In order that this may happen now, we are now today told what will happen to every one of us at the last gate – in order that now, when we are spending our life still outside the gates, this may happen; the knocking at the gate in order to be admitted to full life – the dissatisfaction with our life here, under the call of the Gospel – our dismay at our inadequacy since we are not righteous, and the deep humiliation in the moment of truth, and our protection under the cloak of the one righteous man, who leads us into the land of life. And then, here and now, the new life of gratitude, with innumerable occasions for gratitude in every area of life. That is already a part of the new life within the gate, which flows out into our life here before the gate. Gratitude makes our life whole. For it is true, as the old Bodelschwingh said, "The man who can thank, is healthy".

So, Lord, help us to become whole already in this world and perfectly in the next world, through the gratitude into which you lead us through the message of the great turning unto life.

We have heard the joyful message, Lord, that we shall not continue to be shut out from life, that even our guilt, our failures, shall exclude none of us from life. We hear the message, help us then to believe it and to draw courage from this faith; where we might grow weary, to win faith even in spite of our failure, and to serve you better, courage to struggle even against our despair; help us also to give courage to other people!

Make your Church a fellowship that gives courage to all who wish to do anything for your human race, to give alleviation here and there to the great suffering of this world! We pray to you for our Church here in West Berlin, for those who are harmed by calumny, for our Bishop Kurt Scharf and Undine Zühlke and Cornelius Burkhardt, and correct those who have incurred guilt through calumny, and enable us in our understanding of the Gospel to distinguish between Christian and un-Christian action! We pray for all in authority in our city and in our land, and the two German States, in Europe and in the world. Make them mindful of the responsibility for which they will have to give an account to you! Make them mindful of the task which you have given to them, and help them to find ways towards peace, and ways towards the deliverance of men from hunger and destruction! Give to your people Israel peace with its Arab neighbours! Give peace in Vietnam, bring men in Latin America to freedom, and also in the Soviet Union, and bring together the white and the black in South Africa and Rhodesia, before great bloodshed begins there too!

Help us everywhere to work together to bring about peace, liberation, and reconciliation here in our land, and in the wider world. We pray to you for all on sickbeds, all undergoing operation, all in prison cells, in loneliness, for our old people, but also for our young people who are so often in despair. To all of us, Lord, give courage through the promise that we may go with you from darkness into the light, from unrighteousness into righteousness, from living before the gate in the shadow of death, through the gate that leads to life with you.

Invitation to Joy

Lord our God, joy is what you wish to spread around you among all your creatures, among all men. We are poor servants of your joy. We spread joylessness instead. Through envy and greed we stifle each other's joy, and create suffering and sorrow. We are unserviceable in spreading your joy, unwilling to forgive when guilt meets us, and joyless when sorrow meets us. We pray to you, forgive us that we are so little capable of receiving your joy, and make us new servants of your joy. Lord, take pity on us!

This is the day which the Lord has made; let us rejoice and be glad in it. Save us, we beseech Thee, O Lord! O Lord, we beseech Thee, give us success! Blessed be he who enters in the name of the Lord! We bless you from the house of the Lord. The Lord is God, and he has given us light. Bind the festal procession with branches, up to the horns of the altar! Thou art my God, and I will give thanks unto thee; thou art my God, I will extol thee. O give thanks unto the Lord, for he is good; for his steadfast love endures for ever! Psalm 118, 24–29.

"Joy belongs to faith as a wave belongs to the sea." I read this a few days ago in an article on the word joy in the Bible. And that is quite true, "Joy belongs to faith as a wave belongs to the sea". The pilgrims who sang this ancient hymn of pilgrimage, and knocked on the Temple Gate, and had it opened to them, they had heard that there was a joyful festival in the Temple. They wished to be present at a joyful festival. The invitation in answer to which we have come here, is an invitation to a joyful festival, an invitation to joy. The central word, which accompanies the word God in the Old and New Testament is, though few people know it – the word joy. What we have here is an invitation to joy. Frankly, this sounds strange to us. The world today, this world of ours, is a collection of joylessness, of hindrances to joy, of the gradually growing incapacity of men, as they grow up, really to enjoy themselves, so that someone who is a happy man, is the cause of universal wonder. This invitation of the Gospel "Rejoice, rejoice!" is met with incredulity. How often students have said to me how strange this was to them – really the strangest thing in the whole Gospel – this summons to joy. And they have confessed how incapable they had become in the course of their still short life, really to rejoice. This world is full of hindrances caused by external suffering which stifles all laughter, and full of false ideals and of an avidity for joy which achieves precisely the opposite. Someone may indeed say that after this invitation to joy the conditions must first be fundamentally changed which are such a hindrance to happiness. He would be right. Each of us must play his part in overcoming an order of society which causes so many tears, so much bloodshed and hunger. But the question is, whether it is only the outer conditions which hinder joy. It might be that we had altered them, and still there were no joyful people.

The other question is, what then are we to do? Are we to wait until this world has at last become more reasonable and different? Do we not already today, in the midst of this cruel present time, need joyful people? How do we ourselves become joyful? And what will come out of a change in conditions if it is introduced by people who are full of bad-temper and hate? How can the result be anything less profoundly joyless than our present life? Nietzsche says somewhere in Zarathustra "Since men came to be, man has rejoiced too little. That, my brothers, is our Original Sin".

You remember Jesus' parable about people who are invited by a king to a tremendous feast, and one after another refuse the invitation because they have all sorts of other things to do, land to purchase, cattle to buy, and weddings. Fundamentally this parable of Jesus is a question about the joy in our life, and whether we have an access to joy. Jesus of course does not mean that we could suddenly withdraw from all these activities, purchases of land, and weddings, and everything else that concerns us, trade, and profit and professional life and the news in the papers and elections and so on, and instead could begin a blissful life in the never-never land. Jesus knows that we are involved in these things, and must continue to be so, nor would he at all deny that among these activities some are pleasant. Many of us have the good fortune to be employed in work that satisfies us and daily gives us pleasure. But we know also that that can come to an end tomorrow through some great misfortune, through a bitter quarrel, or through mishap. And we know that a great part of the concerns with which we have to do are but joyless things. Jesus asks for the access to joy. Apart from that we know also that every man who cannot enjoy himself is a burden for his whole environment. A man can correctly do his duty and he can exercise a quite sacrificial love of his neighbour, when he does it without joy, without any rays of happiness shining from him, then the most needful thing is wanting, and he is a mere burden, not a blessing to his environment. And he stifles happiness in his vicinity.

So then it is something very striking and important, when this statement, which in my opinion is unquestionably right, says "Joy belongs to faith as a wave belongs to the sea". That corrects our thought about God, among non-Christians and among Christians. What is the final truth about our life? What is the final power that determines our destiny? The religions and the philosophies try to express in words and pictures our conjectures in this matter. They discover dumb fate, which inscrutably disposes of us, a blind chance which capriciously deals out happiness and unhappiness to us, or the host of gods and powers which quarrel together and compete with each other about us, and all seek to be honoured by us. Or they come to the deep perplexity of "ignoramus ignorabimus" – "we do not know, and we shall never know", which again stifles joy.

The striking thing about the Gospel is that in opposition to all this it claims and declares aloud that the whole world is a creation encircled by profound joy, that it originated in an act of creation which is nothing else than the overflow of eternal joy, and that the will of God is nothing else than the will to help his creatures to enter into a deep joy in life. It is clear that even what Christians have said, and today say, about God in many cases does not yet in any way answer to this; it is frequently a joyless Gospel. But since Gospel means "message of joy", a joyless Gospel is a square circle – a self-contradiction. People have often spoken in such self-contradictory terms in the Christian Church about God. Christianity has been propagated with fire and sword, inquisition and the burning of heretics have accompanied its history, and even today, when that, thank God, is no longer customary among us, so often God is spoken of in such a way that no one could guess that the central word for God in the Old Testament and the New is the word "Joy". God, a despotic super-ego, and religion a compulsive neurosis – that is the faith in God that the great Sigmund Freud heard of from Jews and Christians, and because of this was able to get no idea of the authentic content of the Gospel, the message of joy.

Here in this verse of the Psalm it is all contained. Here men come into the presence of God, and that is for them identical with enjoyment and dancing. *"Let us be glad and rejoice in it."* There people pray to him, and what do they ask for? *"O Lord, help!"* Hebrew Hosanna; English "Set us free!" One must be set free for joy. These people are praying for *blessing*. Blessing is an awe-inspiring word. It means that on a human life there falls a deep, full, all-embracing "Yes". Where there is no blessing, there is joylessness, there is failure, and hence here a request is made for *success* in order that we may be free of the dreadful fear of failure and breakdown, which otherwise always accompanies us. All this is the meaning of *the day of the Lord*, the description of a day of festival, a continuous banquet, which never becomes tedious. It is this day of the Lord in which our faith is consummated. It is already breaking when a little faith is kindled in us. Faith is nothing other than hearing and taking seriously the invitation to joy, and setting it against everything that hinders and stifles faith in us.

Someone among you who knows the Bible well might make a grave objection to what I have said up to this point, an important objection, because it comes out of the Bible itself. He could say "You have only said the half; the Day of the Lord a happy day, and God's nearness as a nearness causing joy". But the Bible has also another story to tell. In ancient Israel there arose a prophet, Amos, who called in to the Temple, to this dancing people that danced its round dances at the Festival of Booths, carrying branches and boughs, and wove twigs of May round the altar: "Woe unto you that desire the Day of the Lord. The Day of the Lord is darkness and not light. Take away from me the noise of your songs, for I will not hear your psalm-singing". (Amos 5, 20–23.) Those who are cried at in this manner, all of us, stand suddenly transfixed, and ask if this has been an illusion, that we have heard and taken seriously; the invitation to joy? Does the Bible contradict itself? Is God after all more of an ill-tempered schoolmaster than the joyful giver of a feast? a sullen despot, a stern judge before whom one must tremble?

When one takes together these two quite different statements about the day of the Lord as light and as darkness, as a happy festival, and as a terrified standstill, then, I think they can both be understood in the light of a question they should lead us to ask, "Who indeed profits by your joy?" "What do other people gain from your joy?" When we consider what the Bible says about joy, we should not overlook that fact that where, as here in the Psalm, the door is open to God's great festival, in the same moment another door is opened to other men. In the same moment when the door upwards is opened and an unconquerable joy can stream into our life, in that same moment the door at its side also is opened.

But now the unthinkable thing can happen, that a man, who suns himself in the warm light of grace which streams into his life from above, through the door between God and him, closes the other door at its side towards other people, perhaps because he feels that there is a draught between the two doors because he is repeatedly disturbed in his pleasure in God by the cries which come in through the open door at its side. It is indeed also possible that this happiness under the warm light of God is much less disturbed, much more contemplative, and edifying, when we close the door to our neighbour. This has often happened in the Christian world; joyfully the door between God and us was left open, guilt can no longer close it, joy streams in. But quietly, or quite deliberately, the door to our neighbour was closed, "God and the soul, the soul and God, beyond this nothing", that is what people then said with the Church Father Augustine. For all their piety, a wall came here into existence; here the possessors of joy, outside the joyless world, here the undisturbed services of worship; (think of that Christmas night Service in the Kaiser Wilhelm Memorial Church), here the undisturbed Christmas night Service, and there the napalm bombs on Vietnam; here the stillness of our piety – and then we go out, out of the Sunday into the everyday, out into the brutal class war of the world, those who have made it against those who have got too little, and meanwhile, the door has been walled up. Only one thing is quite certain, when the door to our neighbours is shut, then sooner or later the door upwards closes through which God's joy streams in. A Christianity that lives only by enjoying God, in the egotistical pleasure of its own blessedness, and closes the door which lets in the draught from our neighbour and the environment, such a Christianity will end by becoming itself narrow and joyless and legalistic. It has attached all kinds of conditions to the joy of God, and cannot any longer proclaim the forgiveness of our guilt unconditionally to all men and invite them unconditionally to the joy of God, and can no longer actively bear witness of this joy to them.

Now, perhaps by using the picture of the two doors we understand what is contained in the word "thanks" with which this splendid Psalm begins and finishes. When I find another person turning towards me, and when this action saves me from isolation, deep depression and joylessness, then one can laugh again with this other person. For you can only laugh with another person – have you noticed that? – when one is alone one can at the most laugh at the memory of shared situations; a Robinson Crusoe alone would in the course of time lose the capacity to laugh. Human laughter is a purely social phenomenon. So when I experience the friendly approach of another person, and I can again be happy with him and laugh because of his approach, then gratitude for this is the most natural thing in the world; it happens of itself. A call to gratitude *"Let us give thanks and be glad"* is not really necessary. An injunction, "But you ought to be grateful!" when a schoolmaster with raised forefinger reminds us of our duty of gratitude, often spoils our gratitude. The real meaning of a call to gratitude is "You should open your eyes and acknowledge what has happened to you in this man's friendly approach, then you will be grateful and laugh". It is a call to acknowledgement, so this call "Let us give thanks and be joyful!" is a call to acknowledge the friendly approach which has been made to us, God's friendly approach to us.

There are always two movements in gratitude, in feeling and in action. Gratitude has always two dimensions, our inner and our outer life. Gratitude has always two organs, our heart and our head for feeling and thinking in us, and our mouth and our hands and our outer bodily life in acting our gratitude. Gratitude has always two directions. Therefore gratitude has always two words, "Thankyou" and "What can I do for you?" "I can be glad" and "I may help". Gratitude is accepted when the person whom we thank, lets us share with him in his work. Gratitude is really expressed, when the one who is grateful interests himself in the work of the person whom he thanks.

Thus gratitude needs two doors, one opening upwards and one opening outwards to men. The man who has no door upwards is stifled, then his piety is joyless, without gratitude Christianity is a paralysed, tired Christianity, where we indeed still stiffly and wearily sing the hymns of joy, because they have a place in the traditional liturgy, but tend to be irritated, as has happened when other people outside, for very enthusiasm about the newly discovered message of joy, start to dance, as happened in the Liturgical Night at the Kirchentag in Düsseldorf in 1973. When our gratitude does not also go through the other door, towards other people, then it gradually dies, because it has no interest in the work of the One I am thanking, my thanks are nothing more than a weary obligation. The work of him whom we thank, is to spread joy. *"Thy goodness endureth for ever."* Your love endures for ever, and it is our privilege to share in spreading God's joy. *"O thank the Lord, for he is good, and his steadfast love endureth for ever."*

Forgiveness and Mission are One

In the year that King Uzziah died I saw my Lord sitting upon a throne, high and lifted up; and his train filled the temple. Above him stood the seraphim, each had six wings; with two he covered his face and with two he covered his feet, and with two he flew. And one called to another and said: "Holy, holy, holy, is the Lord of hosts; the whole earth is full of his glory". And the foundations of the thresholds shook at the voice of him who called, and the house was filled with smoke. And I said "Woe is me! For I am lost; for I am a man of unclean lips, and I dwell in the midst of a people of unclean lips; for my eyes have seen the King, the Lord of hosts!"

Then flew one of the seraphim to me, having in his hand a burning coal which he had taken with tongs from the altar. And he touched my mouth, and said; "Behold, this has touched your lips; your guilt is taken away, and your sin forgiven". And I heard the voice of the Lord saying, "Whom shall I send, and who will go for us?" Then I said, "Here I am! send me". Isaiah 6, 1–8.

"In the year of King Uzziah's death I saw my Lord" – not any Lord, not one of the many Lords that have to rule over us, not any god, not one of the many gods who lead their existence in our world, but him, "the Almighty Lord" as some translate it – I saw him, the highest, the one Ruler of all, the principle of all principles, the last reality, that which one cannot see as one can see every other thing, but that which all our questioning and investigation and intellectual efforts strive to reach, the first origin, the final goal, and the power that rules over all.

"I saw" – there was no obstacle, no concealment, no wall between us. I came into the field of clearest knowledge. Nor was I drunk, not "high", as if under drugs, not dreaming, but in a state of normal, but clearest consciousness; so it was that I saw the last reality.

Truly I saw still at a distance, from below, not yet "face to face" – not more than just the fringe of the garment of the final truth and the highest reality, but that in itself is more than what we can reach with our sharpest efforts of thought and most daring thrusts of investigation. I saw; that means that I stood in the closest, most immediate encounter with God.

This is what we strive for, and long for, what the prophet experienced, without our being able to reach it. But there is an advantage in this. We envy those who are able to tell us of such visions, such extraordinary experiences of God, such encounters with the final reality, and would like ourselves to share in such experiences. But do we know what we are asking for? Do we then know beforehand what that would mean for us: whether life, and not death? This man here, carried up to the heavenly Temple, into the realm of final truth and clarity, does not say "How wonderful that I am permitted to experience something like this!" But rather, "Terrible, the worst thing that could happen to me! Would that I had never come here". *"Woe is me, I am lost!"*

This means however, that man and truth – these things do not go together; they contradict one another like lying and truth. Man and God – these things do not go together, they contradict one another like death and life. That is very vividly shown in this vision; the world of light of the angels, the eternal joyful song of praise, the riches of the earth that joins in with this song of praise – the whole universe one expression of God's joy – and in the midst of it only *one* being that must cry out "Terrible! That is my death. I am not created for the truth, not for the light. The light kills me!" *"Woe is me, I am lost, for I am a man."* So then man would be the damned creature in the Creation, created by God in anger, therefore excluded from true life and light, he intolerable for God, and God intolerable for him? But this man sees himself *not* annihilated by the encounter with God because he is a man, but because he is *"a man of unclean lips"*. It is not his humanity that hinders him from joining in the great song of joy and praise to God. That is precisely the destiny for which he was created, to be the image of God on earth, he is destined to be the mouth of the whole creation in this song of praise. It is an impurity, a darkness, an untruthfulness, an opposition which prevents him from being this. It does not come from God, from the creation, but entirely from ourselves. An opposition to God, to true life and light, and therewith also to our own being and our own destiny. The whole of human life and the whole of human history are signs of this profound alienation from God and from ourselves, our highest soaring thoughts as well as our deepest falls, the élite of men as much as the ragged proletariat, what we do in war just as much as what we do in peace.

The Bible in fact believes that things would be just the same with every one of us, as it was with this man Isaiah, confronted with the final truth, with the divine life which fills the creation, every one of us is stripped of all agreeable self-deceptions, and must acknowledge himself as the dark blot in the creation, that must be removed in order for the creation to join with clear and pure voice in the great joyful hymn of praise of the angels. That is for us the intolerable truth, which we try to disguise from ourselves with all kinds of inventions, a truth which we face when the Word of God touches us.

A miracle happens, the miracle of all miracles, that this impure being, impure in the midst of the pure creation, that this intolerable being is permitted to live. The annihilating encounter with God becomes for him a life-giving encounter. Without his co-operation, entirely on the initiative of this other power that ought to have meant his death, that which must be death for him is turned into new life; the miracle of forgiveness. He who can no longer purify himself is purified. *"Your iniquity is removed, and your sin is covered."* Death is taken away, the death which I bear in myself because of my contradiction, my impurity is covered by the encircling life-giving love to him who was the prey of death.

My hope is based on nothing less
Than Jesus' blood and righteousness;
On Christ the solid rock I stand
All other ground is sinking sand.

When I come to the light of the final truth that is unbearable for me, –
"If God is for me, who will be against me?" I am allowed to live.

What does life mean? Life means – now we know this, life means
praise, to be permitted to join in the great hymn of praise of life and
truth – the great hymn of praise to God. Before, the word was – so also
we may translate the Hebrew sentence which I rendered by the words
"I am lost" – "*I must be silent*". The man of unclean lips cannot join in
the hymn of praise. But when there is no longer anything that prevents
us from joining in this, no accusation and no question, above all, no
contradiction, no guilt, no anxiety, no bad conscience, no death in us,
no fear of death, no condemnation to death – when our life is merely an
act of praise, then we really live, and so far as now – in spite of
accusation and question and guilt and anxiety and fear of death, we live
under the forgiveness of God, and take it as more serious and real than
everything that tells against it, so far our life is already a real life, freed
from death.

What does life mean? Life means something further, which is most
directly connected with the first thing, with life as praise. For with the
miracle of forgiveness the story has not yet come to an end. Forgiveness has silenced our deadly questions; we can praise again. But now
the forgiving God asks us a question, an astonishing question. God,
who has need of no one, who is dependent on no one, the God who is
eternally rich, God "the omnipotent" – needs someone. He needs
someone who is there for him, who goes for him out into the world,
who brings to other men messages from God. God asks, seemingly
without knowing what to do, seemingly asking for help and helpers for
his cause, "*Whom shall I send, who will go for us?*"

The astonishing thing after this astonishing question; someone
answers; the very same person answers who but a moment hence
seemed entirely a lost soul. The one who, in the light of truth, a
moment hence knew himself to be the most useless creature in the
whole creation, the same dares to consider himself useful, to announce
himself as serviceable. "*Here I am, send me!*" And the answer to
this is not "Are you crazy? Forgiveness has surely turned your head!
Be glad that you are forgiven, and do not imagine that therefore you
are serviceable". No, the answer is *Mission*. The miracle of forgiveness is followed by the miracle of mission, forgiveness and mission
are indeed *one* miracle. Forgiveness and mission are two sides of the
same thing, of the allocation of life. One might say that forgiveness is
the form, and mission the content of the allocation of the new life. "But
where there is forgiveness of sin, there is also life and blessedness"
as Luther's Small Catechism says.

But what then does life mean? Life means to have a content, a meaningful content for one's life, something for which one lives, something which it is worth living for. This man Isaiah now receives something for which it is worth while to live, is worth while, even if it costs him his life. Forgiveness means to live from God, and mission means to live for God, and forgiveness is the permission and empowering to live for God, the power to live an eternally meaningful life. At first you may find it meaningful to live for your profession, your family, your nation or for the progress of mankind, but perhaps also to live only for yourself and your pleasure and enjoyment of life. All that will someday come to an end, all that will be repeatedly eroded by the doubt of meaninglessness. To live in the mission of God, for God's cause, is eternally meaningful life, and it is this also which brings into life for your profession, family, nation, for the really so necessary progress of mankind, and into the hours of your pleasure and enjoyment an indestructible meaning.

What then is the cause of God? The purpose of the whole Bible is to give us an answer to this question, by showing us how in quite different times, in quite different situations, quite different people came under the message of forgiveness and were shown how God does not desire the death of men, but their life, what the true life of men is, and how they can contribute to this true life of men round about them. By this we learn to know which pursuits serve life, and which serve death, where we can advance something that is friendly to life, and must renounce and resist what is hostile to life.

This can lead us into very hard conflicts, as at once happened in the case of this man Isaiah. If you go on at home to read the second half of the chapter, then you will see that with this new meaningful content of his life, life will become, not simpler, but incomparably harder for this young Isaiah. The message of life that he has to bring is in his case a hard message of judgement. It is not without intention that he begins with the date, *"In the year that King Uzziah died"*. Everyone, who read that, knew at once, that was the last year of a period of peace for Israel, that lasted fifty-two years, a time which later generations looked back on with longing. Just as many people in our times long that there might be once again such a long, peaceful, beautiful "good old time" like that between 1870 and 1914, and so perhaps coming generations will some day long for thirty such years of peace as we have now undeservedly had since 1945. In this year, the last year of King Uzziah, Isaiah – that is his first task – must announce to unsuspecting Israel that now judgement will fall upon the nation because it has not used this long time of peace to serve God's cause, to be a blessing to all nations, to create justice in its own midst. That was, as if a prophet in 1912 had been forced to stand up and predict to the nations of Europe the judgement of blood that was now coming upon them, because they had not used the time of peace for the blessing of the nations of the earth, but had enriched themselves with the madness of armaments, and colonialism, and exploitation of the nations. Or if he had then in 1912 said to the Christian Churches what would happen to them, and what first has happened to the Churches of East Germany and Eastern Europe, not that we should receive it, and look at it with clenched fists, but acknowledge it as a judgement of God on a Christian Church that has mistaken the God that created iron for the God of Abraham and Isaac and Jacob. Or, it is as if a man in 1976 were compelled to stand up and proclaim to the peoples of the white industrialized States the judgement of God in blood and horror towards which they are going, because again they have only used this time of peace for the folly of armament and exploitation, and not for the blessing of the starving peoples and the oppressed masses of the earth. So the life of the messenger becomes a hard path. So the mission can bring us into conflict with what men round about us are striving for and defending with all their power.

So the mission can make us lonely, as it made this Isaiah lonely. If we Christians do not come into conflict with the greed of position and the madness of armaments, and the conditions of exploitation around us, then the suspicion is that perhaps we are only enjoying forgiveness, but refusing to commit ourselves to mission. The joy of forgiveness is inseparable from taking mission in earnest. To take mission in earnest, we are promised, leads to real joy, for to be permitted and empowered through forgiveness, to live in God's mission, to be permitted to share with others in serving God's cause, God's concern for mankind, and God's will that his mankind should have life, that alone is the eternally meaningful life.

You, our Lord, you speak to us through the Prophets, whom you have enabled to see the truth clearly. We pray to you, let us also recognize it, forgive our disloyalty, and bring us to share in your mission, in life that is true life.

The Catastrophe as Turning Point

I was invited to expound a word from the Prophets for a volume of sermons by Jews and Christians which is shortly to be published, and it seemed to me that this word I have in front of me is the right one for us to hear today.

"Therefore I will judge you, O house of Israel, everyone according to his ways, says the Lord God. Repent and turn from all your transgressions, lest iniquity be your ruin. Cast away from you all the transgressions, which you have committed against me, and get yourselves a new heart and a new spirit! Why will you die, O house of Israel? For I have no pleasure in the death of any one, says the Lord God, so turn and live."
Ezekiel 18, 30–32.

It was exactly 30 years ago, on May 11th, 1945. We lay in a Bohemian meadow in the May sunlight, chewed stalks of grass, and spoke about the future.

The nearer future, whether we would succeed in crossing the Moldau and escaping captivity, and the further future, what would happen to Germany and all of us.

While we chatted thus, a Sergeant Major rose, a big, powerful man who up to then had sat silent, and went over the meadow into the forest. Immediately after, we heard a shot, and when we ran to him, we found him, already dead. The comrades of his group, whom we had met accidentally, said that up to now he had had unquestioning faith in the Führer, and in the days since Hitler's suicide had only said one thing "Better dead than a slave".

So for him the catastrophe was an end-point after which nothing more worth-while could happen; and so his only wish was to die. A catastrophe can mean three different things:

1. It breaks in upon us and strikes us dead; the catastrophe as end-point.
2. We raise our heads again, discover to our astonishment that we are still alive, creep out again, and start again where we left off; the catastrophe as interruption.
3. We hear a signal, an ultimatum; things cannot go on as before. Right about turn! A complete change of direction! The catastrophe as turning-point.

But catastrophes are dumb. We must draw out their meaning, and tell ourselves what it is; they themselves do not tell us. For this reason, at all times, prophets rise, false prophets with false interpretations, and true prophets. But who can distinguish rightly between them? A true prophet is a man to whom illumination is given, to help him to set events in their right light, and to help men draw the right conclusions from the events. In times of catastrophe we have bitter need of prophets, of true prophets because we have bitter need of the right conclusions, men of vision, who spread illumination around them. So today, let us listen to a prophet of old times, who proved to be a true prophet, and discover – let us listen to it carefully – that what he said then to his people in a time of collapse may be just as illuminating to us today!

He proclaims the catastrophe as God's ultimatum, *and* as an offer of great liberation, as a turning-point. Here it is clear how false the alternative is, "liberation or defeat". Of course 1945 was a defeat, a terrible defeat. When a criminal regime collapses – 1945 in Europe, 1975 in South Vietnam – then it buries beneath it in its fall innumerable guilty and innocent people. As then the Churches of the Confessing Church in which we had received strength to resist the power of evil, were destroyed by bombs in exactly the same way as the Churches of the German Christians and the Temples of the Brownshirt State Worship, then we had to learn that when God's judgement falls on the evil ways of a nation, neither God nor men will make a neat selection according to good and bad, and that those who gave warning by no means come safely out of it and remain unscathed. They have all some part in it, we were all in some manner involved, and shared responsibility and guilt, we must all bear the consequences. We have had to learn that. Of course a defeat is dreadful after so many years of war, after so many victories, after so many sacrifices, after so many atrocities; we had to face this. We had to learn that in the many conversations here in Dahlem, in which we realized that in this war we did not have any *right* to wish for victory for our people, but must wish for this dreadful result, defeat, for its own liberation!

What the prophet says is a challenge of the living God, who transforms the defeat into a liberation, the end-point into a turning-point. The first, *you are allowed to go on living.* And, indeed, we are allowed to go on living. We survivors, we who sit here, and among us the survivors of Israel, who escaped from our annihilating fury, we are allowed to go on living, although what then lay before did not seem very worth living for. After bad years of hunger, we were satisfied once more, more than satisfied. Towns and villages shine as new. Both the German States are stabilized economically and politically, and no longer threaten each other, but are coming gradually into normal relations with one another. And also we do not wish any longer to threaten the neighbours around us, and we are less and less felt by them to be a threat. So it is not too rash to believe that the centuries of wars within Europe are at an end, and that Europe has become an area of peace in an unpeaceful world. This is owing to a new way in politics, which at long last, gradually, for some people too gradually, has been entered on, and for which we will be grateful. For that is the second message that God's challenge contains. *"Turn from your offences."* Catastrophe as turning point means also a turning away, unsparing self-criticism, breaking with the old bad traditions, knowledge that the catastrophe was not a natural disaster, not a blow of fate, not merely the result of the regrettable superiority of our enemies. The German catastrophe did not begin in 1945, it began in 1933 with jubilant enthusiasm of the masses, in our commitment to the doctrine of the master race, might rather than right, persecution of the Jews, the Führer State, to preparation for war, to the programme of suppressing other peoples in the east. And this catastrophe did not fall from heaven, it came from old bad traditions, in which our upper classes and the Churches have had more share than the workers. Traditions of death, bringing death to others, and in the end bringing death to us.

"Why will ye die?" – this is what the God of Israel asks his people, and his question was unheard as he saw how among us here evil traditions were preached from Church pulpits and in Universities and schools, and evil seed was sown.

"Why will ye die?" – the Gospel asks us this today – it is *the* question of the Gospel everywhere, where it is heard in the life of every individual, in every nation. Of the first world war the philosopher Max Scheler said that it had been an ultimatum of God to the nations. All the nations and all the Governments failed to hear this ultimatum, above all we Germans, and the result was the second world war. It was God's new ultimatum, his last in the great world order. For the third world war will leave no trace of us behind. The new efforts that were made in the thirty years since God's ultimatum were in part too insignificant, in part too half-hearted and inconsistent, and in part only an attempt to go further along the old paths with new methods, in order not to have to pay the price of catastrophe. We sit in a world of atomic armaments at our Sunday lunch-tables, surrounded by the millions of the world-hunger catastrophe. The nations have since then undertaken several wars, running the risk of a world conflagration. We have a share in the destruction of the landscape, and the squandering of the wealth of the earth, by means of which we are making the world uninhabitable for our grandchildren. When a people tries to free itself from our exploitation, it is bombed to pieces as in Indo China, or filled with torture chambers and concentration camps as in Chile. We are still in love with the ways of war, we still believe that we can win our life at the cost of other peoples' lives, and that is the road to death, which can lead to nothing but death for us also.

"Why will ye die?" – that is the question that the God of Israel puts today to his people Israel, who escaped from our gas chambers, and are permitted again to live in their land, and asks it to devote all its energies to make peace with the Arabs.

"Why will ye die?" – that is what he asks the Arabs, and requires them instead of this thousand-fold death and mutual murder, to accept the Jewish state in their midst, and receive them as a member of the family of nations in the Near East.

"Why will ye die?" – he asks us rich industrial nations, and commands us urgently to cease building our prosperity upon the exploitation of the rest of the world.

"Why will ye die?" – he also asks the peoples of the socialist camp, and compels them to realize a socialism which is combined with demo-

cracy and freedom, in order that the rest of the world may learn new ways thereto.

"*Why will ye die?*" – so he asks the Christians in all the lands. They ought to know better. They have received from the Gospel the vision of a new manner of life, a new society, in which some no longer live at the expense of the others. They are the messengers of the new way of life among the peoples. But the Christians and the Churches have in many cases gone along with the old ways of life with class exploitation, and national wars, with oppression and contempt for other races and peoples, and in addition given to it a religious veneer. We Christians, above all, stand before God's ultimatum, which is at the same time an offer. "*Get yourselves a new heart and a new spirit!*" That is no longer impossible. Away with the unbelief of resignation that says "We are old men, we are leaves written upon, none of us gets a new heart and a new spirit, that is a pure utopia". Just as truly as the new man Jesus Christ has died and risen again for us all, so truly is that possible for us, and it is our fault if it seems impossible for us to leave the old ways of death for new ways, to build nuclear cells with new spirit and new heart, with living radio-activity in all nations, which radiate power, and help the nations to find ways into a life that will no longer be won at the cost of others, but in which new orders of society will encourage a solidary communal life, and nature will no longer be destroyed by our careless exploitation.

"*Repent, that ye may live!*" By hearing that, and beginning to do it, we say that to others also, and help them by our action critically to test their traditions, to reject what in them is productive of death, and to move forwards towards a life of solidarity.

In this Christian Protestant Church we are today present together as a thoroughly ecumenical community of mankind. Protestants, Catholics, Jews, Buddhists, atheists from the Soviet Union, we are sitting together in a brotherly manner, and hearing the same call of the God who is there for all men, for the atheists and for the Christians, and for the Buddhists, and for the Jews, and perhaps – I don't see any – there is also one of our Moslems among us – if there is, he is very welcome! Today the same thing is being said to all. Once more a thirty-year-old war has now come to an end, the war in Indochina. After the terrible news from Chile in 1973, there came in the years 1974 and 1975 the joyful news of the opening of the doors of the prisons and concentration camps in Greece, in Portugal, in Mozambique, in Angola, in the tiger-cages and the prisons and concentration camps in Vietnam.

As in 1945 I went into captivity, a Soviet soldier in Vienna told me in the railway station of the terrible things he had seen at the liberation of the concentration camp at Mauthausen, and while I was travelling to Russia into captivity, my heart could still be full of joy about the people from Mauthausen and Buchenwald, and Bergen-Belsen and Dachau and Auschwitz and all, that they were now out of captivity. We know quite soberly, that every liberation on earth is only partial, and liberations are repeatedly conjoined with new injustices. This must not hinder us from rejoicing, but it must at the same time be an incentive to hear this call of the Prophet *"Turn and get yourselves a new spirit!"* Permanent revolution of heart and spirit! That is what the Prophet calls to every people whose representatives in this place we are, to every group, every religion, every world-view, as the ultimatum and the offer of God for the sake of all mankind in the year of new beginnings 1945, in the year of new beginnings 1975.

The Horizon of the Eternal Mercy

And Mary said, My soul magnifies the Lord, and my spirit rejoices in God my Saviour, for he has regarded the low estate of his handmaiden. For, behold, henceforth all generations will call me blessed; for he who is mighty has done great things for me, and holy is his name.
Luke 1, 46–49.

For the three sermons which I am to preach today, in December and in January, I have chosen the so-called Magnificat, Mary's song of praise in Luke's Gospel – an Advent text about which, however, we will begin to think today, before the beginning of Advent, on Eternity Sunday, which draws our attention to the last questions, to death and life, to our origin and goal and purpose. Do not think that our text is not suitable! Certainly, one can say of every section of the Bible that it fits Eternity Sunday, the Sunday of the Dead, as it used to be called, for every section of the Bible is spoken and written *sub specie aeternitatis*, in view of eternity – and that always means too, in clear knowledge of our temporal character, the limitation of our life by death.

This is specially true of Mary's song of praise, and, indeed, though it does not speak about death and dying, but only, and triumphantly, of life and fulfilment. But it does speak of a life saved, and thus not of life as a secure possession, that cannot be lost, but of a life threatened by death, which can only rejoice because a "Saviour" appears to it, a deliverer, when God becomes its deliverer.

God the deliverer of life – that is indeed a theme for the Sunday of the Dead and Eternity Sunday, a very necessary one, because we carry in ourselves the life that is condemned to perish. We are going to meet our death, and we see it everywhere around us, in the old people who often travel so wearily and with such great burdens towards their last days, and today so often in the case of young people, whose life seems to them so lost that they throw it away because they do not believe it possible that this life of theirs might be a rescued life – and finally and especially we see death when we look out into this world of nations armed against each other with the most horrifying weapons of death, and watching each other intently.

The ideas that many people associate with the word "God" seem in no way to help here, quite the reverse. If we ask the great thinkers, then they point us away from time into eternity. "God" is the name used to describe the last inscrutable and ineffable ground of all finite beings, and God is the great horizon that surrounds us, and that includes all things in himself, but in a way inconceivable for us. And just at that point all thought about God begins to grow despairing. For there we have immeasurable eternity – and here our tiny existence which passes in a moment; there is the Eternal Ground – and here is the onset of cancer, the suicide of a beloved child, the cry of a tortured man – and we do not know how that fits together, and how it could have a meaning under this great horizon. Our suspicion grows ever greater that it might have no meaning at all, the great horizon of God might surround us in vast, eternal, indifference, as indifferent as the nature that surrounds us, and in the end receives us back into itself in corruption, as if we had never been.

Eternity, the universe, God – or whatever you may call it – that is so great, and I am so tiny, so unimportant, so lost in face of this greatness. Here too, in this Psalm, which Luke's Gospel puts in Mary's mouth, there is that contrast; the great God and insignificant man. But here that is not occasion for a complaint that we are lost, but an occasion for exultation. How does that happen, and how can we also come to this point?

The key-word is the sentence: *"He has regarded the low estate of his handmaiden"*. The woman who says this has heard something that annuls and bridges over the antithesis between that dreadful, indifferent greatness and our insignificance. She has heard a word from this eternity that was hitherto so dumb, so indifferent, a word that changes everything. Eternity is looking at me. It can look at me. Its eye is directed to me, a puny, transitory, lost creature. What surrounds me then is not the cold, eternal, dumb and blind abyss of nothingness into which I shall shortly sink. A personal interest out of eternity directs itself to me, I am important, not unimportant to Eternity. Eternity concerns itself about me. Eternity loves me as itself, Eternity is in reality the living God.

Truly this is something quite inconceivable, with inconceivable consequences for our existence. Truly it is something unbelieveable; one can perhaps dream of it, but can one also believe it, that is, rely on it with absolute certainty? For this reason no one has dared to say it with certainty, no religion and no philosophy. Among all the seekers for God and those who think about God in mankind, there stands the little band of men of the Bible, the Prophets and the Apostles, and God's people Israel and the Christian Church, and among them also the young Jewish woman Miriam, and in the midst of these people of the Bible, Jesus of Nazareth, and they all say it with certainty to us in our lostness, contradicting our apparent lostness, "The Eternity that surrounds you is the living God. He can see, he can speak, he can hear, he can love, he can do battle, he can conquer, he can save – and he is looking at you".

In Biblical usage "to regard" is more than to see. Nearly thirty years ago a striking film was showing "The Third Man", which contained the following scene. From the top of the tower in the Prater in Vienna, two men who are planning a great crime are looking down on the crowds of people swarming below. And one of them says to the other. "What does it matter if a number of them perish? Destroy a hundred, a thousand of these people down there, and it will never be noticed, there are plenty of them, they will continue swarming; the individual is unimportant in this great crowd." That is the philosophy of the great ones of the earth; it has enabled them repeatedly to look down on the crowd of little people on this earth, and to send them into their wars, and today those great ones are preparing methods of mass destruction for the others. The great Napoleon gave expression to it when someone referred to the thousands who had fallen in one of his battles, and he answered contemptuously, "Pah, in one night Paris begets just as many new ones!" But the Book of Job tells us of the living God, "Behold, God is mighty, and does not despise any". (Job, 36, 5.) "To regard" in the Biblical sense, is to be understood, as a mother regards her child, as two lovers regard each other, they see in each other their happiness, their wealth, they give their life to each other, they are willing no longer to be without each other. The puny human beings who cannot give anything to the eternal and rich God, these are the people whom he regards, it is they whom he chooses to share his wealth, without them he is not willing to live, for them he pledges his life, and indeed for every single one among us. For him there are no masses, for him no one is lost in the crowd, for him it is not only the crowd that is important, in order that he can use it for something, for him it is not only the whole of mankind that is important, for him every individual part of mankind, even the most insignificant, is important, for him everyone of us is his beloved "Thou".

And more, among the insignificant, among all men, to him the most insignificant, the undistinguished are obviously especially dear. The living God is drawn to little people just as we are drawn to fine people. His direction of movement is quite contrary to ours. Martin Luther describes this contrast in one of his finest writings, in his exposition of the Magnificat (1523). "This is our daily experience, how everyone strains only after honour, power, mastery, the good life, and everything that is great and high. And where there are such people, everyone attaches himself to them, everyone runs to them, everyone serves them gladly, everyone wishes to be there and share in their greatness, so that it is no accident that in the scriptures few kings and princes are described as pious. Again, no one is willing to look into the depths, where there is poverty, shame, distress, suffering and anxiety; there everyone turns away his eyes. And where such people are, everyone runs away, people flee from them and leave them, no one thinks of helping them, of standing up for them, and making people consider them; so they have to remain in the depths, and in the base despised crowd. There is here no creator among men who is willing to make something out of nothing, although Paul says and teaches (Rom. 12, 16) 'Dear brothers, do not be haughty, but associate with the lowly'."

These things have not changed since Luther's times. Among us too there is this thrust upwards, this wish to be important, this belly-crawling before the mighty, and it is taught, with or without *numerus clausus* to children also, and countless neuroses show how sick people can for this reason become through feelings of inferiority and failure. If we did not live in contradiction to God's will, but in the same direction as God's will – and that means, regulated our conduct by God's, then we would be free also to take the part of the little people, as it is said in this Psalm about God's behaviour. And that means simply this, to do to others the same kind of thing that makes our own life worth living.

For this is the central proposition of the Gospel. Our life is possible because others are merciful to us, other people and the living God. It is indeed dinned into us in our acquisitive society, that we live from what we have earned for ourselves by our efforts, and in the class society it has always been dinned into us that the higher a man stands through birth or good fortune or his achievements, the more he can claim from life, and the more he has of life. But the life that one gets with this is, accordingly, possessions, money, honour, which indeed flatters us, all that indeed, but that is only a shallow substitute for life. We begin to come to life, really to live, when others are merciful to us, and are there to help us, not because we might repay them, but simply because they are not willing to leave us alone, because they wish us to share in their life. So the child lives from the mercy of its parents, so younger people live from the mercy of older people, who do not wish to keep their experience and knowledge to themselves, but to give it to the young. So the older people live from the mercy of younger people who do not hold it against them that they are becoming old-fashioned and weak and stiff, do not despise them for this, but respect them as those who preceded them in the way of life and on the way to death which they also will have to travel. All human life together is then a life-giving life in fellowship, when it is lived in mutual compassion. And just so do we respond to God's life with us, we repeat what God does, and thank him by this repetition, "behold God is so great, yet he despises no man".

It is well known that Martin Niemöller once said that men were today less troubled than in Luther's time by the question "How do I find a gracious God?" and more troubled by the question "How do I find a gracious neighbour?" That is very true. But now also we can realize that neither of these questions can replace the other. They belong as indissolubly together as do the command to love God and the command to love our neighbour. To seek for the grace of God, and to rejoice in the grace of God without being a gracious neighbour to our fellow-men – is pure egoism. See Jesus' parable about the wicked servant! This means the condemnation of all unpolitical Christianity, which seeks to confine itself to religion and does not take any part in translating gracious neighbourliness into social structures which help men to life rather than withholding life from them.

But the converse is equally true, by being merciful to one another, by acting as gracious neighbours we can give much to each other, help each other much, but always in a very limited and fragmentary manner, not only because unfortunately each one of us is still more concerned for himself than for another, but also because we cannot prevent others from being, like ourselves, insignificant human beings, at the mercy of forsakenness, the deadly abyss of nothingness, the final meaningless-ness in the horizon of an indifferent eternity. When this horizon, stony and dumb, surrounds us and engulfs us without mercy, then we shall not be able to do anything more with our mercy for our fellow-men, we have then enough to do to keep ourselves going and to care for ourselves. Having pity on myself then leaves me no time and power for taking pity on my fellow-men. But when the horizon of eternity becomes the horizon of the everlasting mercy, when the love of the living God who seeks men cares for me, insignificant transient man that I am, then the message of the gracious God makes me free to be a generous neighbour. Then even the prospect of age and death no longer makes me anxious and self-seeking. He has looked with loving condescension on my low estate, and in the same way he looks at every one of my fellows, and when I look at every one of my neighbours in the same way, then I am in harmony with eternity, then my life praises the eternal love, and thus lives in a world that has eternal meaning.

The Psalm is put by the Gospel writer in Mary's mouth. Of course it does not come from Mary herself, nobody stood beside her then with a shorthand notebook. It is a means chosen by the narrator to make clear, right at the beginning of his Gospel, what his whole narrative is about. In appearance Mary is speaking here only of herself; she seems to be speaking of a fame which she herself will achieve. But if we listen more closely, then she is referring to an event of which she herself is only an instrument. *"All generations shall call me blessed."* Not because all generations, that is, all of us, will envy her because of a grace that comes only to her. No, we call *her* blessed, because through her *we* have become blessed, not through her merits, through her innocence, through her immaculate conception, through her holiness, and whatever else people have invented in false honour done to Mary, but because of that of which she became an instrument. Her rejoicing comes from this, that she has become an instrument for a regard of God that is directed to the lowliness of *all* men, for God's participation in the life of us men of low estate, of low estate through our insignificance, death and guilt; for the miracle of God's self-giving which entered into our life, for the miracle of the Incarnation of the great eternal God in our human brother Jesus of Nazareth. She gives us by her rejoicing an example for our rejoicing, which will stay with us in suffering and death, the more we recognize ourselves all as men who, all together, every one of us, with every one of our neighbours, have been looked upon by God through our brother Jesus Christ, and this regard is the salvation of our life.

God is the Revolutionary

And his mercy is on those that fear him from generation to generation.
He has shown strength with his arm, he has scattered the proud in the
imagination of their hearts, he has put down the mighty from their
thrones, and exalted those of low degree; he has filled the hungry with
good things, and the rich he has sent empty away. Luke 1, 50–53.

The Magnificat, Mary's hymn of praise, together with the lily of the
Annunciation angel, the flute music of the shepherds, and the angels'
Gloria belongs to the emotional context of Advent and Christmas.
And beautiful as that is, and not to be despised by a people that has so
little capacity for festival and celebration as ours today – this context
has also the danger that such ingredients are thoughtlessly employed
merely to produce a mood. But if you listen carefully to this hymn of
Mary, as if it were for the first time, then it strikes you how little it fits
into this emotional context, because it does not seem to be speaking of
the things that are mentioned in Advent, even in genuine Christian
preaching.

Let us assume that one of us had to compose the hymn of Mary, how
would it go? If Augustine or Gerhard Tersteegen had been given the
task, they would have concerned themselves entirely with God and the
soul, with the soul and God. Martin Luther would have rejoiced over
the "blessed exchange"; God's Son takes on himself the guilt of sinners, and gives the sinner his righteousness. Similarly, Karl Barth
would have written that God goes into the deepest abyss of humanity,
and by so doing lifts our humanity to his divine height. But, strange to
say, the evangelist Luke takes quite a different line. He leads our
thoughts neither to our inward experiences of faith, nor to the great act
of God in Jesus Christ, but outward to the real history of men and
nations, to world history and politics, to power-relationships and social
questions, to hunger and revolution – indeed to all the things that we
simply don't want to hear about at Christmas, as was shown at Christmas in 1967 when Rudi Dutschke tried to remind the worshippers in
the Kaiser Wilhelm Memorial Church about the war in Vietnam, and
was indignantly thrown out for doing so.

That Luke here is using an already existent Psalm which comes from
some pious Jewish group, and that this Psalm goes back to the Psalm of
Hannah at the beginning of the First Book of Samuel, which expresses
the same kind of views, is no satisfying explanation. The evangelist
who, as modern scholarship carefully notes, has thought a great deal
about every stage of his narration, must here also have acted with clear
intention. It ought therefore to be made quite clear from the beginning, that the words and actions of Jesus, and finally and above all his
death and resurrection, have not only to do with the relation of the
individual soul to God, nor yet only with God's salvation for "all"
mankind, by which something still very abstract might be understood.

Jesus' coming has significance for the real history and the real struggles
of men, for national wars and also for class wars, just as here the wars of
men, as if we were reading the "Communist Manifesto", are exclu-
sively described as class wars.

At first you can read this description without taking sides, quite
neutrally, and you will find in it exactly what old citizens of Berlin are
more aware of than young ones, when they go to the castles at Charlot-
tenburg or Bellevue, or make an excursion to Sans Souci. A Berliner
who is seventy-six today saw as a child of twelve with his parents the
officers riding in the Tiergarten, the parades from the Brandenburg
Gate down the Unter den Linden, and at the Court parties admired the
dress uniforms, and on an excursion to Potsdam tried to get a distant
glimpse of a member of the Kaiser's or the Crown Prince's family. So
firmly established seemed this splendour, and only a few could imagine
that in a few years the saddler's apprentice Ebert would be the head of
State, and that the gigantic Russian Empire, would be ruled from the
Kremlin, with its priceless art treasures, not by the Tsar, but by a
committee of proletarians and revolutionary intellectuals. It is to be
understood that Conservatives, for whom the dynastic order was an
order of God's grace, saw in these revolutionary changes only a revolt
against God, and thought that he who is for God must be against the
Revolution, and therefore a counter-revolutionary!

But in so doing they must have listened carelessly to the Magnificat,
which they heard at least once a year in Advent. For here it is expressly
stated, *"He has put down the mighty from their thrones, and exalted
those of low degree"*. He led Ebert into Berlin Castle, and Lenin into
the Kremlin. He brings it about that in such revolutions starving
proletarians fill their stomachs in the larders of castles, and rich people
fall into the direst need – all this experienced time and again in this
century of revolutions, and probably not for the last time.

So here in the first place we are compelled, not at once to declare the
revolutions as being directed against God's will, but to see God's will at
work even in the revolutions and through the revolutions. It might be
the case that the counter-revolutionary himself was the rebel against
God, such as he believes the revolutionary to be. God works in history
not only as the stabilizer of orders, as the Conservatives see things, but
also as one who overturns orders. The man who is stricken and destroyed by such revolutions should remember the hard, and for us so
offensive word of the prophet Amos, "Shall there be evil in the city,
and the Lord hath not done it?" and it can help him in his misfortune to
say with the stricken Job, "The Lord gave, and the Lord hath taken
away, blessed be the name of the Lord".

Does that mean then, that we should simply cooperate with such
revolutions, or indeed that we should always fight on the side of those
who are succeeding in the overthrow of an existing order of power?
Are *they* always in the right, on God's side, whether their name be
Lenin or Hitler or Pinochet? Are we to take the modes of our action
simply from history and its successes? Should the Christian stand in

principle on the side of revolution, instead of on the side of the existing order, as the Churches have mostly taught? We shall find the answer to such questions when we ask what can the words of this Psalm have to do with the coming of Jesus Christ, of which they do not expressly speak, but to which they doubtless relate.

The coming of Jesus Christ is the revealing of the will of God; in the neighbourhood of Jesus Christ it is bright between God and us, between us and God. Otherwise everything is still in darkness, and the concealed will of the "concealed God" lies also in darkness, as Luther put it, that is, the question what this "up and down", this rising and falling, with all the horrors that are connected with it, can have to do with the will of God, with the goodness and wisdom of God. Through the coming of Jesus Christ there is light now already, even in the midst of the darkness. There is light now, firstly because we may believe and hope that God's good and gracious will stands behind everything, even behind the misfortune, and may thus receive comfort and power even in the days of misfortune and the prospect that when we see him face to face, we shall praise him for everything saying "You have done all things well". And secondly, because now we are permitted to see what God wishes us to will and to do, because we can know the direction in which he wants to set us in movement as his co-workers whom he has won by his mercy.

But this direction of God's will can be quite clearly recognized in the verses of our psalm. It is written there, not only as we have already read, that God ever and again throws everything into confusion, and the changing spectacle of history that we at all times observe, is his work. What is said here is not only what stands in the hymnbook;

God's wondrous works have won renown,
He raiseth up and casteth down,

but here God's words are spoken of with special emphasis. The whole class society, rolling forward through all revolutions through thousands of years to the present day, is brought before our eyes. There are the mighty on their thrones of power, while down below are the great masses, and the mighty have at their disposal the riches of this world, and the masses below them vegetate in a life of naked misery, and the mighty pretend that this disorder is God's order, and use religion to legitimate their power, and to hold those below in subjection. That is how it has always been, and Christianity has also been used to justify this.

But he, who in Jesus Christ comes on the scene in the midst of this class world history is not willing to be the God who will be at the beck and call of the power and riches of the powerful. This so-called order is not the order that he wishes for men. His heart beats for those who are at the mercy of the powerful, and to whom life is denied, who go away empty or dissatisfied in the distribution of the good things of the world. And that means, not only that he consoles them in their poverty, that when earthly goods are denied to them, he gives them a compensation through spiritual, heavenly riches, and the prospect of his Kingdom in the future or in heaven, in which there will be neither rich nor poor. That is what the Churches have always said to the poor, and that was not wholly false, that holds good for all the poverty on earth which we cannot alter. But there is more in this text! Whether we like it or not – please do not accuse me, as if I wished to preach now my political views from the pulpit – accuse the Bible, from which my political views come! – here without question our eyes are directed to earthly goods, and it is proclaimed that God will do something here on earth in relation to earthly power and earthly wealth. He will overthrow this so-called order which is disorder, and see to it that the oppressed are exalted and the hungry are fed – indeed, one can translate literally the Greek word that stands here, "will be able to fill their bellies with good things". This too – and not only the forgiveness of sins and the justification of sinners – belongs to God's justice; God for the underdog!

We will not now ask how he, our God, brings to fulfilment in history this will of his which has been revealed in Jesus Christ. We will only ask how far this indicates a direction for our action. For what we, as disciples of Jesus do, when God's will becomes clear through Jesus Christ, is also a means whereby God fulfils his will in history. And it is about us that these verses are speaking. If we have become disciples of Jesus, then we may apply the first verse of our reading to ourselves. *"His mercy is ... upon those that fear him."* "To fear" does not mean to have fear, but rather to have respect for the master of their life, to let him give direction to that life and action. For them the promise of his mercy is of the greatest importance.

The struggle for a share in the wealth of this world is a merciless struggle. In revolutions a merciless judgement is passed on those who hitherto were powerful and rich. But the reason for this is, that the order they maintained, with its injustice, was no less merciless – a fact that we often forget, when we shudder aghast at the horrors of revolution, and do not see the misery and frequent death that were previously caused by the power of the powerful and rich. Those who "fear him" are people who know his mercy, live from his mercy, and no longer from what they can snatch for themselves in this struggle for their share of wealth, and therefore they are no longer partisans of an interest-group which is set on having or holding on to something, but rather, like the merciful God, who takes the side of those that have been unfairly dealt with and gone under in this merciless struggle. It is they who are to be first considered before the revolution, and equally after it. And then the aim must be that this whole struggle for a share in the distribution should stop, or at least should be moderated as much as possible. For they see how in this struggle everyone is dehumanized, the rich and powerful just as much as the underdogs who are trodden down and hungry. So those who fear the Lord take part in politics, not as fighters for their own interests, for their own advantage in wealth, but in the direction of God's now revealed will for the lowly and hungry, with the aim of making the struggle less merciless, by means of better laws of production and distribution, and replacing it, as far as possible by a better order. That is *"from generation to generation"* the true chain of God's men here on earth. And truly they have special need of God's *mercy*, God's sympathy, help and care, because this will bring them into deep conflict, into conflicts with themselves, that is, with their own interest in earthly wealth, and into conflict with all those whose greed for power and wealth they threaten by such action. But by doing this they are following Jesus Christ, who went before them on this path, in this direction, and who suffered a like fate, and who, as the Risen One says to his disciples the Advent word, "I will never forsake you on this path, I am coming to you" (John 14, 18). Even so, come, Lord Jesus!

New Life in the Old World

He has helped his servant Israel, in remembrance of his mercy, as he spoke to our fathers, to Abraham and to his posterity for ever.
Luke 1,54–5.

Some years ago, in 1969, I took part in a television discussion between representatives of the great world religions and the world outlooks about the problems concerning the future which confront us today. A member of this group was Roger Garaudy, hitherto the chief theorist of the Communist Party of France, who a few days previously had been expelled from his party on account of his too great independence of thought. My Jewish colleague, Professor Werblowsky from Jerusalem, and I had spoken of God's covenant with men, and I had summarized the confession of the Christian faith in the sentence, "Man and the world are not alone", adding "God is the name of the one who has committed himself to me". Garaudy set against this the sentence, "For me an atheist is a man who acknowledges that man bears the full responsibility for his history. That means: we atheists have no promise, no covenant, and no one is waiting for us" (cf. Marietta Pelz, (Publisher) "If we wish to survive". "World Confessions answer Contemporary Problems", Munich 1972, 203–215).

This then, in our land, where Christians and atheists live mixed together and work together, even when they make good efforts for this troubled and threatened and self-destroying race of ours – this is what often makes us seem strange to one another. The Christians say "We have a great promise, and in our human history we are not alone; there is one who co-operates with us, who has promised to attain his goal in this history". And the atheists say: "Of that we know nothing, of that we see and hear nothing, we are entirely on our own, we men make our history alone, and no one is helping us to reach the goal".

Now, granted that we Christians are not in the position of having the message in our pockets, so that we could take it out and hit the atheists with it on the head to prove our superiority. Often we ourselves have doubts about it, and it sounds to us like a fairy story from the ancient times. Often we ourselves go ahead quite atheistically through life, as if we too were quite alone and left to our own devices. And on the other hand we repeatedly meet with people who call themselves atheists, and who at the same time are moving in a spirit of complete self-sacrifice along the paths into which we have been directed by God's will revealed in Jesus Christ, as we heard in the last sermon on the Magnificat. Thus the distinction between Christians and atheists becomes relative; it is by no means a distinction between us as better men and the atheists as worse men. And yet there is still a difference, and that is the difference between the tasks which result from these different outlooks. We hear the promise, and we must pass it on to those who feel themselves left alone and wholly dependent on their own resources in a meaningless infinite world. It is this promise of God that is the theme of the Magnificat. In the last sermon we found the content of the divine promise and expounded it. Today we must ask who are its recipients, and secondly, how it is fulfilled in Jesus.

Who comes to hear this promise, to whom is it addressed? Mary's hymn, at its close, narrows our field of vision; starting with the great story of humanity, it concentrates our attention on a small section, a small group of people, on Israel. In all his work for the great goal of humanity, mankind in the Kingdom of God, God does not forget his little people, who in the Bible are called "the apple of his eye". Indeed, in everything that God does for the whole of mankind, there comes to fulfilment what he has promised to this little people, "his servant Israel".

Thus this little people has firstly a significance for mankind that no other people has, and secondly we cannot speak of the Gospel, of God's coming to us men in Jesus Christ, without speaking of Israel, and this not only for the reason that, since mankind is divided up into peoples, he must come to the world in one or other of its peoples, as if it were only by chance that it was the Jewish people, and not the Greeks or the Chinese, or as we would perhaps like it to have been, the German people. No, it was for a deeper reason, from the inmost necessity, that Jesus is Jew and not Greek, Chinese, or German. It comes from the necessity of the divine promise, from the connection of promise and fulfilment. Right at the beginning of his narrative, the evangelist insists to Christendom: you cannot have Jesus without Israel, – and if Gentile Christendom had not thoughtlessly misread this, then it would not, in the course of subsequent centuries have burdened itself with such terrible guilt against the Jews, the descendents of Abraham.

Israel is the people that in its ancestor Abraham was privileged to hear this promise of God for the whole of mankind. Through this Israel became a people of hope unlike any other people in the world, looking forward ever more, ever more intensively, and hoping for a future time of fulfilment, a time of liberation, a time of the Kingdom of God, a messianic time. Israel is the *Servant,* that is, the people chosen to serve the divine promise. Israel is the community of Jesus Christ, chosen long before his coming through God's covenant to be his community, to be his brotherhood, witness to his promise in the whole of mankind, which turns so hopelessly on its own axis in self-torture, a place of faith and hope and liberation in the midst of the darkness and chaos of the history of mankind. Anyone who wishes to belong to the community of God on earth, must belong to Israel, to *"Abraham's seed"*. That was the great discovery of the first Christian community after Easter and through Easter. It consisted of Jews, and it discovered that now also the Gentiles were permitted to belong to it, might be received into God's Abrahamic community, and share in its witness to the great promise of God for all mankind.

We can of course ask, why is the promise not at once made known and audible to the whole of mankind? Why do there continue to be people who with Garaudy sadly say "Nothing has been promised to us, we hear no promise". Why has only a small part of mankind been chosen to hear and to bear witness, when this is meant for all mankind?" But here too, the principle holds good: our why-questions for the most part are not answered here on earth, they are transformed into questions asking "for what purpose?", and *these* are answered for us. For what purpose are these few people privileged to hear? As *representatives,* says the whole Bible, they are privileged to hear as representatives, in order that they may take up the message into their lives and live a joyful, confident, hopeful life under the promise, a new life, and this not for themselves alone, in order that they may have it good, while the others continue to wander around in darkness. No, it is for the sake of the others that they are privileged to hear it, in order that they may spread abroad the light to the others. God wishes to bring the light to men by means of men, and therefore he chooses men for himself, and gathers them together into a community through their common hearing of his promise, and by so doing calls them light and salt and leaven for the whole of mankind.

Through this great calling to be representatives, Jews and Gentiles who believe in Christ, Israel and the Church, belong together as bearers, witnesses, and messengers of the light of promise as God's servants to the whole of mankind, and right at the beginning of the message about Christ, the Church is told by this verse of the Magnificat, that it must not isolate itself from Israel, or indeed stand against Israel. Only together with Israel does it belong to Jesus, because Jesus inseparably and first belongs to Israel. For the coming of Jesus signifies that he, the God of Israel *"has helped his servant Israel in remembrance of his mercy"*.

But precisely at this point there arises, up to the present day the difficulty between Jews and Christians, which becomes evident when at the end of our study of the Magnificat we ask "How then is the great promise of God fulfilled, and how is the coming of Jesus the fulfilment of the great promise of God? In his Stories of the Hassidim, Martin Buber tells how once a crazy man on the Sabbath got hold of the great Schofar trumpet and blew it as it will be blown when the Messiah comes. While everyone hurried in alarm on to the street to receive the Messiah, a wise rabbi looked out of the window, and said "This is not the hour of deliverance", and remained in his room. So at that time after Easter, the Jews heard Jews in their midst cry in triumph, "He is risen, he is risen indeed", heard them cry in triumph that the Messianic age had begun, looked out of the window on the unchanged world, and declared, "This is not the hour of deliverance". Thus the difference and contradiction among those who still belong together to God's people of the promise made to Abraham has remained to the present day.

Be honest! Is the behaviour of the Jews not more understandable than the exultation of the Christians, of the New Testament? We have already sung that we have received that light which has driven out of the world so much fear and pain, that nothing dark can here remain (Evangelical Church Hymnbook, 51, 3). Is that true? Plenty of dark things have remained since the earthly days of Jesus. The world is full of them, everyone experiences it in his personal life; in the two thousand years since then, mankind has not suffered less than in the preceding millennia, and it seems to many today that the Apocalypse of John was nearer the truth when it pictured how mankind would not have to suffer less but ever more terribly.

But this same Apocalypse of John, which is a very relevant book today, and, as a matter of fact the last book of the New Testament, and the whole Bible, is not a Jewish, but a Christian book. The author does not say Jesus may have been a great prophet, but he was not the fulfilment of the promise made to Abraham. He says instead, – and here he differs from the Jews – Jesus is the fulfilment of God's great promise – and he says with the Jews that the suffering and sinning of men continues, and the deliverance lies still before us, and the whole New Testament says so too. How are these things compatible; the fulfilment has come already, and the deliverance has not yet come? What has changed through the coming of Christ, and what has not yet changed?

I think that the answer of the New Testament to these urgent questions can be summarized in one sentence. The deliverance has not yet come, but the Deliverer has already come. Sin and death are not yet done away, and that means, that men still kill one another for the sake of earthly wealth, they still have "proud heads and hearts" (v. 51), the powerful still sit on their thrones of power and tread others down, there are still satisfied rich men and hungry poor men, still sickness, old age, bereavement and loneliness of all kinds plague us. *But* he is already "with us on the scene with his Spirit and his gifts". He has already bound himself to us indissolubly in Jesus. The victorious battle has already been waged on the Cross and made secure, so that destruction, wickedness, the devil and death do not have the last word, but life, light, and the promise of God. There is not only a promise for a distant future. He fulfils already the promise in the midst of the unchanged world through liberations now, through fellowship with God now, so that now we do not merely hope for eternal life, but again and again experience new life, and can bear witness not merely to the future of a new life at the end of the old world, but to the presence of the new life in the midst of the old world – and on these grounds can go forward into a stronger hope. So within the one people of God which embraces Israel and the Church, we reach forward together with our Jewish brothers towards the final coming of the Kingdom of God, and must nonetheless say to our Jewish brothers "We are already permitted now to say more and to witness more than the ancient fathers before Christ were able to say and to witness. The Kingdom of God is not only in the future, it is also in power in the present, we do not merely hope for the forgiveness of sins at the Last Judgement, but it has already been given on Golgotha, and we are already living in its power. The Spirit of God is already poured into our hearts through the Gospel and liberates us for actions of love in individual life and in politics. Death has already lost its power, and we are able to sing resurrection hymns at gravesides."

We may and should already on earth create at least the beginnings of new relationships in which the mighty are cast down from their thrones, in which human servitude is ended, and the hungry are filled with good things – this all as evidence for the fact that the coming Kingdom has already begun to take shape on earth. For the Redeemer has already come, and through his battle on Golgotha and his Easter victory, has created facts which death and the devil and even our blindness and lack of faith cannot undo. The victorious Redeemer is on his way to the final perfect redemption – and it is our privilege to be with him, to see that in faith, and in fact stand beside him and be instruments of his present power. If we take to heart these words "The Redeemer is already here", then we shall realize that the witnesses of the New Testament and our hymns have not overstated it. We too, if we wish to do justice to what happened in Jesus, cannot say less, cannot express ourselves more modestly, with more reserve. And the more we take this to heart, the more new power we shall receive to fight everything that contradicts God's promises, that contradicts the Redeemer and the Redemption, and stands in our way. We shall become witnesses and bearers of the light in the midst of this world that is still so full of darkness.

God be Gracious to us Christians

He also said this parable to some who trusted in themselves that they were righteous and despised others: "Two men went up into the temple to pray, one a Pharisee and one a tax collector. The Pharisee stood and prayed thus with himself, 'God, I thank thee that I am not like other men, extortioners, unjust, adulterers, or even like this tax collector. I fast twice a week, I give tithes of all that I get'. But the tax collector, standing far off, would not even lift up his eyes to heaven, but beat his breast, saying 'God, be merciful to me a sinner!' I tell you, this man went down to his house justified rather than the other." Luke 18, 9–14.

One of the oldest manuscripts to which we owe the text of the New Testament, the so-called Codex D, omits in the introductory verse of our text the word "parable". That is certainly no slovenliness, but a conscious omission, by means of which the copyist himself indicates that he does not consider this story as a parable, but as a real story, whether observed by Jesus himself or not, certainly to be taken literally. This itself is a first indication that in hearing this story familiar to us all, we should avoid a misunderstanding which one can find everywhere in commentaries and sermons. It is the opinion that this is a parable which represents to us two kinds of people at prayer, in order that we should avoid imitating the unattractive example, and behave like the example worthy of our imitation. This conception is so much the easier to accept, as the parable understood in this manner makes sense; a humble man, modest and self-critical, is more attractive to us than an arrogant one, who preens himself on his righteousness, and we may rightly conjecture that he is also more attractive to God. But if this were the meaning of the story, then the real Pharisees would have had no need of Jesus' instruction. In their utterances that have been handed down to us, are also to be found some which praise repentant humility in God's presence, and censure self-satisfaction, and these real Pharisees were by no means conceited and self-righteous people, or even people with only a semblance of religion – a meaning which, unfortunately the word Pharisee has in general use among us modern men – a usage of words which has partly arisen from the misunderstanding of this story. But still more important; if the story were to be thus understood, the tax collector would have gone down to his house "justified" rather than the Pharisee for this reason, that he as the humble one was the more religious than the other, and his humility, his unsparing self-knowledge and its open confession would then be his achievement, the fulfilment of a condition that is necessary for being justified, and we would once more be faced by a law; thus you ought to be, and thus you ought to pray, and if you are not like that, then you will not be justified. And, true and useful though an exhortation to repentant humility is for us all, even if we do not understand it legalistically as a condition of our justification, still I believe that I see that this story does not contain a law, but a splendid Gospel, that Jesus wishes to bring home to the Pharisees with whom he is speaking.

A small observation already points us in this direction; the tax collector beats his breast. He does not dare – Jesus says – to approach the Temple, or even to enter it, he remains standing far off, perhaps even in the "Forecourt of the Gentiles", he feels himself because of his guilt and his unworthiness excluded from the people and fellowship of God, and deservedly so, and he does not dare, as people used to do, to raise his eyes or even his hands to God, but he uses his hands to beat his breast. But that is not a gesture of prayer. People beat their breasts who wept in despair over the body and the grave of a beloved kinsman, in grief and despair. People beat their breasts who were condemned to death and entreated for mercy. Thus the words of the tax collector, in contrast with those of the Pharisee are not a prayer, but an outburst of despair, and an outburst of despair is nothing that one could set up as an example to follow. For one can wish to imitate an example, but not an outburst of despair. One is held by despair against one's will, it is a situation not wished by us, but a very real one out of which we have to be delivered, or in which we shall perish; in despair we cry for help. In despair the man condemned to death cries to the judge to have pity on him.

Jesus speaks with the Pharisees who believed themselves to be just or as we can simply express it, respectable people, and he makes no attempt to deny that they are so. One may even doubt whether his picture of the praying Pharisee is so critical as we are accustomed to think it. What Jesus looks at critically is something else, namely that, apart from the conviction that they were respectable people, and apart from their very necessary thanks to God for this, that he has helped them to be so, they feel contempt for other people who have not succeeded in attaining such respectability and righteousness. We all repeatedly catch ourselves harbouring such contempt, and especially when we are concretely and infuriatingly and painfully confronted by the disreputability of other people. Jesus makes the Pharisees look at this tax collector, and shows them what happens to him in the moment of truth, i.e. when he no longer succeeds in defiantly and frivolously deceiving himself about his condition, but when it dawns on him that by his behaviour he has excluded himself from a true good life, and how inescapably in time and eternity he has incurred the just judgement of God. Although he is a Jew, he has become a treasonable functionary of the Roman tax system, by means of which his people was bled to the last drop of blood; perhaps he became this out of necessity, as recently did the poor sons of peasants in Nicaragua who allowed themselves to be recruited for Somoza's National Guard in order to obtain a livelihood and privileges, and thus became enemies of their people. He has been hopelessly entangled, perhaps he has a family, which he has been able to save from need by sharing in the exploitation, and when he comes out, then his employers will take their revenge on him, and his people will not receive him again because he is too much compromised by shame and injustice. He does not know where to turn, and knows that he is rightly despised by all who have not allowed themselves to be lured into his treasonable action, God's reality has all at once dawned upon him, but it has dawned upon him as a terrible, killing reality, and therefore he stands now so far off, beats his breast, and cries for mercy.

It is this man whom Jesus makes the Pharisees see, and at the same time makes them see God in a new way, as the God of immeasurable love who also embraces this lost creature of his, and will not cast it away, but save it from its destruction. This immeasurable love is the sinner's "justification", the turning of God in help towards one from whom all turn away in contempt. God looks at him as his child, whom he is not willing to give up, and does not count his guilt against him, or hold it up to him, but desires to help him out of his shipwrecked life to a new life. Jesus does not tell us any more about the tax collector, he does not tell us how this turning of God, this justification of God took effect on him, how he became aware of it, and how he was able to go on living with it. That is not necessary for his intention, for his whole purpose is to make clear to the Pharisees, the despisers of men, how now through the immeasurable love of God, a new hope shines over the ruined life of this man, and how radically new a vision this can give them of the God whom they so earnestly desire to serve.

But Jesus never shows us a new vision of God in order that we should merely have new thoughts about God. He wishes to give us new thoughts about God in order that our behaviour should change. When we allow ourselves to be shown by him the reality of God's love that seeks men and sinners then our behaviour will alter in two ways.

First. We consider these Pharisees, and all of us, in spite of our imperfections, to be – on the whole – respectable people who do not despise God's commands. For that reason they and we are easily inclined to despise people who live contrary to God's commands. But the longer we and the Pharisees look at the tax collector, and watch him go back to his house in the hope that Jesus has given to him, we will find the whole contrast becoming questionable, which hitherto we thought that we could draw between such contemptible people and ourselves. The question will penetrate the certainty of our righteousness when the moment of truth comes for us, and God's reality stands as threateningly before us as now it does before this publican. We shall be asked whether we have not incurred the divine judgement just as much as the people whom hitherto we have despised. We will begin to examine ourselves in a way we have never done before, or have carefully avoided. We shall discover, alongside our advantages, great causes for dubiety, which hitherto we have overlooked and behind our advantages perhaps an abyss of egoism, lovelessness and calculation, so that our pride utterly collapses, and we see ourselves unexpectedly standing beside the tax collector, like him without any justification on which, after such a stringent examination, we can still rely. And in such a collapse of our self-security we shall only be able to cry pitiably *"God be merciful to me a sinner!"*

So, standing side by side with the tax collector, we shall also ask if we ourselves are not the guilty causes of the contemptible character of this contemptible man. What have we contributed to making a man such a greedy traitor, an exploiter of his people, and a cut-throat, like this tax collector, and to making other people *"extortioners, unjust, and adulterers"*? What have we perhaps contributed to this by doing nothing against conditions in which other people believed that only by collaborating with those who robbed their fellow-men they would be able to survive? Have we perhaps only protected our greater respectability from infection by them, by carefully avoiding contact with them? If this is the case, then our righteousness is nothing better then a great egoism, and then we owe our respectability only to the ruthlessness which makes us abandon the others to their depravity and enables us to cultivate our piety and virtue for ourselves in the sheltered circle of the devout? Then we have not imitated God's all-embracing love, but given expression in our lives to a quite restricted love, confined to good people, and basically entirely selfish, and we ought not to expect with this to be acknowledged by God as righteous, as people who please him.

Or on the other hand, what contribution do we make to the life of these other people with the advantages that we have over them, and for which we rightly, like the Pharisees, thank God? I mean, what do we contribute by our difference from them, whom we despise as unjust, with our faith and piety, and our life according to God's commands, and our prayer and churchgoing? How are we helping to bring these *"other people"* out of their bad life and condition, and so out of their despair? When we regard our advantages – as the Pharisee rightly does, as a gift of God, and thank him for them, have we used these gifts as the giver intended? Have we placed them in the service of God's love to these lost and despised people? Have we gone with these gifts in a spirit of help to the lost, as Jesus does, instead of keeping ourselves from them like lepers, in order in self-defence to nourish our arrogance? "What is not service, is robbery" says Luther. It might thus be that we, who do not consider ourselves as robbers, are exposed as robbers, dishonestly holding on to God's gifts and misappropriating them for our own use. God does not receive thanks for any gift without at once asking us "What have you done with it?" "How far have you served my love for which the others, the despicable ones, also seek?" What have *the other people* profited from the fact that beside them were living people to whom, as to you, so much faith and piety and virtue have been given by God?

Christoph Blumhardt, that incomparable witness to God in Swabia in the last century, preached on the same eleventh Sunday after Trinity in August 1891 a sermon on this text. In it he was concerned with these questions. But he did not, as I have done thus far, and as is customary,

concern himself with the behaviour of individuals. Being a man of the
Kingdom of God, who concerned himself with the universal, for him
the Pharisee and the tax collector were a picture of the history of
Christianity to the present day. He saw the Church and Christians in
the role of the Pharisees, arrogantly exalting themselves above the
"other men", the heathen and the Jews, the atheists and the commu-
nists, sunning themselves in the splendour of their higher religion, their
higher culture, and their higher ethic. But he saw on the other hand
how this Church and we Christians will fare when God passes judgement not only on the others, but on us too, when he takes account of
our way of life and our failure, when he relates our way of life to the
misery of which Christians have brought to other people, often in the
name of Christianity and God; the extirpation of the Indians, and the
enslavement of negroes, the burning of heretics and witches, the
atrocities of colonialism, the crusades of past days and war armaments
of today in defence of Christian culture against its enemies, and the
simple fact that we, the so-called Christian peoples of Europe and
America, take possession of the greater part of the world's riches for
our prosperous way of life, and the rest perish in hunger and misery
and tyranny. When the moment of truth comes, then we shall move
from the place of the Pharisees to the place of the tax gatherer, and
then it is we Christians who will beat our breasts in despair, "God, be
merciful to us Christians!"

And thus at last, says Jesus, at last you are right with God: not so
long as, like the Pharisee, you thanked God for God's gifts, but left the
others in the lurch, or even despised them, did nothing for them, and at
the same time deceived yourselves about your superiority. But now,
when you recognize the truth, the truth of your failure, the truth that
you especially, beyond all others, have played false with God, and then
in despair, because you can find no other means of escape, cry "God be
merciful to us Christians!"

Then we are right with God. Then he has got us to the point where
we no longer in arrogance and self-righteousness see ourselves standing above other people, and either despise and reject the *"other
people"*, or wish to dominate them and shape them to our model. Then
we become of use to serve his love that seeks men out, then we shall
invest our gifts, for which we thank him, to this end, and discover new
possibilities, better than hitherto, to live with and for other men. And
may what Jesus says to us through this story help us to do so!

Part Two

Reason at Last, of Another Kind

The next day Jesus decided to go to Galilee. And he found Philip and said to him "Follow me". Now Philip was from Bethsaida, the city of Andrew and Peter. Philip found Nathanael, and said to him, "We have found him of whom Moses in the law, and also the prophets wrote, Jesus of Nazareth, the son of Joseph". Nathanael said to him "Can anything good come out of Nazareth?" Philip said to him, "Come and see". Jesus saw Nathanael coming to him, and said of him, "Behold an Israelite indeed, in whom is no guile". Nathanael said to him, "How do you know me?" Jesus answered him "Before Philip called you, when you were under the fig-tree, I saw you". Nathanael answered him, "Rabbi, you are the Son of God! You are the king of Israel!" Jesus answered him "Because I said to you, I saw you under the fig-tree, do you believe? You shall see greater things than these." And he said to him, "Truly, truly, I say to you, you will see heaven opened, and the angels of God ascending and descending upon the Son of man". John 1, 43–51.

In 1930 I conducted a short series of evangelistic meetings for the Confessing Church in a Thuringian village. On the invitation cards issued we had written the fourth verse of our text. *"Nathanael said to Philip: Can any good thing come out of Nazareth?" Philip said to him, "Come and see!"*

In the discussion a local Elementary School Teacher protested violently against this verse, and against what I had said about it. "We Germans of today reject the advice to go to that place and to see, to go to the land of the Jews, and to a King of Israel. We have realized that the Jews are our misfortune, and we have realized the significance of race. We no longer seek salvation among the Jews, but in our own people, in our own nationality, and with the Führer who has arisen in our midst. And for that reason we shall fight against the Church to the last drop of our blood, and thrust it aside, because it entices us to seek for our salvation in something alien, and not in our own race and in our own powers."

I can still see vividly the young man in his enthusiasm standing before me. Perhaps he too was among the fallen, and perhaps today those whom he left behind him, on this day of national remembrance, are thinking also of him. But in what manner? All sorrow, all revulsion at the murder of human beings in the wars of our century, is only fruitful and has an effect on our life, when sorrow and horror result in repentance; a turning away from the wrong path into which that teacher had allowed himself to be enticed, and into which he wished to entice his pupils, a way which today we all bitterly regret, a renunciation of the weapons of death with which we plan to destroy others, in order to preserve for ourselves what we call life, and what is only a postponement of death. A turning towards a new way in which we learn to live at peace with other men, choosing rather to suffer injustice

73

than to do it – a way in which we can free ourselves from the atheism, the godlessness of our deadly armaments race, in which even we Christians are today involved, and come to a true faith in God, whom we daily deny with our atomic weapons, a faith in the living God. He alone can preserve our life and make it worth living. Without his will, not a hair will fall from our heads. It was his love that gave us life, and in his love we pass at death into his eternal life. It was faith in our race and in our Führer that made us men of death. This faith in the living God will make us men of peace. By entrusting our life to him we become free from the deadly fears which make us enemies of our fellow-men, free for a peaceable life with other men, free to wish them well, and to oppose with single-hearted zeal the weapons of terror with which east and west today confront each other.

How do we know that above us there is not empty nothingness, and that a dumb fate does not rule over us, but that over us and around us is the living God, to whose hands we may entirely entrust our life? A light has shone into the darkness of our deadly conflicts "The light shines in the darkness" (John 1, 5). It comes from a man in our midst, from him whom men in our history *"find"* – like people who stumble on in great darkness and who do not know whether at the last they will come to ruin. Then one of them suddenly sees a light, and calls to his fearful comrades in suffering, and to those who do not believe it, or do not see it, or do not trust the light, he can only say the one thing that here Philip says to Nathanael, in answer to his question of doubt: *"Come and see!"*

"What good thing can come out of Nazareth?" Nathanael had asked. He lives in Cana, an hour's journey from Nazareth, and perhaps he despises the people from Nazareth, as it is often the custom for the people of one village to speak contemptuously of the people from the neighbouring village. But chiefly because from his schooldays up he has learnt from his Bible that salvation comes from Jerusalem, from Zion, but certainly not from a hole like Nazareth in Galilee. His question has been repeated through the centuries up to this day. The messengers of the Gospel have gone all these years to all the peoples, and proclaimed the light "All you who are in the darkness, we have found the light with which one can live, the longed-for light which the prophets have promised!" "Where, where? We see nothing, darkness surrounds us, darkness without light." The answer is the name of a man from a Galilean village, *"Jesus, Joseph's son, from Nazareth"*.

No wonder that this does not make people jump to attention. It did not then, nor does it today, when we have in addition to contend with the passage of time. Yet it is strange enough, really, since this conversation between a few village people in Galilee, the New Testament and all Christian witnesses have done nothing else but point, with arms outstretched, and with the highest claims, to this one point, to this one man, Joseph's son, who shortly afterwards was tortured to death on a gallows in the capital city of salvation, in Jerusalem. Has he changed the world? Has the world become better in these two thousand years? Has he brought the Kingdom of God? If he *was* a light, has it not long since been extinguished, at least, has it not lost its power?

In the question of Nathanael there lies irony, mockery, conceit, and today it has acquired in addition a tired, hopeless sound. "What good for us can come out of Nazareth?" "People have already preached Jesus to me, and I made a stab at it, but nothing happened. Here, in my case, and in my environment, everything would have to change visibly before I could take an interest in him." The question of Nathanael is the question of all of us. Very often not a genuine question that waits for an answer, but a rejection in the form of a question, a conceited "Impossible, that is too absurd, all the evidence, all world history contradicts it!" In addition our pride comes into play, as it did with the Thuringian teacher; "A Jew out of that hole in Galilee! No! then we would do better to trust our own powers." And so the teacher speaks for all of us. For, even if we have today repudiated as dangerous nonsense the Nazi world-view into which he let himself be conned, yet the final conclusion of our wisdom is also, that faith in Jesus Christ is a beautiful edifying thing for Sunday morning, but that on weekdays in the realities of this world we do better to rely on our own powers, setting realities always against realities, and do better to rely on our own armaments than on the armament of faith. Against Soviet rockets, Jesus and faith are no good, the only things that can help us are NATO rockets, every sensible man knows that!

But what kind of reason is this; the reason of the godlessness of the working day, that reckons with everything tangible, with export statistics, and rocket statistics, but not with the living God, whom the so-called Christian nations and the so-called Christian parties confess only with their mouths, but not in their practice? Kaiser William II and the German General Staff calculated rationally in 1914, and made a wrong calculation; Adolf Hitler, with his rearmament, made, as most Germans then thought, a reasonable calculation and mis-calculated; the Americans in Vietnam made a reasonable calculation about the intervention in Vietnam, and were wrong. Now NATO makes a reasonable calculation with the middle-range rocket; rearm now, arm in order to keep up, and only then disarm. Is there not a high probability that once more there will be a frightful miscalculation, and the result will be the opposite of what was striven for, annihilation, widespread murder, death instead of life?

Reason at last, of another kind! That must be our word today. Where things that were held to be reasonable continually turn out to be most unreasonable, could not what seemed unreasonable be reasonable? *"Come and see!"* says Philip, whose eyes have been opened, to Nathanael and every one of us. Come and see this Jesus once more as he is. Come and take him seriously, the way that he wishes to take you, take faith and discipleship seriously. It could be that something turns out to be reasonable which you will not regret, like the things which seem to be reasonable. It could indeed be the case that those who recommend him to you do not deceive you as your so-called reason and your teachers and leaders have deceived you.

As Nathanael takes it on himself to speak with Jesus and to listen to Jesus, his eyes are opened: *"Rabbi, you are God's Son, you are the King of Israel."* What does he perceive? He sees this son of Joseph no longer as a feeble man like all the rest of us, but as the presence of the living God in our midst, and he sees God no longer as a mere idea, or as a Highest Being far away in heaven, but as a reality on earth, on whom one can count. He sees Jesus as *"King"*, that is, as one who has power, however concealed, a power that is able to cope with every other power. He sees him as one who can be trusted in life and in death. He sees him as one whom I must stand by as a subject stands by his King, as one with whom I must work; with whom it is worth while to co-operate. To this decision Nathanael remains faithful from now on, as John the Evangelist tells us (John 21, 2); he remains his disciple even through the terrible story of the sufferings of this King, and the risen Christ confirms his belief that it is good to trust this King, and to let nothing deter one from discipleship.

For he perceives that this Jesus is a programme for life, the programme for a new life, a new way, a new practice. The disciples of Jesus break with the old practice and its semblance of reason; life is a struggle for existence, we must be stronger and devour the rest, otherwise we shall ourselves be devoured.

That is the practice of death. With this godless practice the nations are destroying themselves; with it we have brought mankind to the brink of the abyss today, and unless a spirit of repentance grips us, it will in the next years celebrate new and fatal triumphs.

In his "Word for Sunday" Heinrich Albertz recently said – to the anger of self-styled Christian politicians: "The older I become, the more I am convinced that Jesus' Sermon on the Mount makes much more sober, practical judgements about this world and us men than all the political and military programmes." That is true. The recognition of this truth, and the practical action it entails must then be expressed in political action. We must set the rationality of the Sermon on the Mount over against what appears to be reasonable, but not only by challenging the Government, but by ourselves resolutely entering on the path of discipleship, and further, by entering into the political discussion; and challenging in a spirit of profound scepticism the rational arguments for rearmament and seeking to refute them by reasoned arguments, and by spreading abroad a spirit of peace which makes it possible for the other side, in this case, the Soviet side, to co-operate and to initiate measures "that will create trust", as men put it, in the present debate about armaments.

In this matter it is decisive that we, for our part, have made the resolute decision: I, a disciple of Jesus, do not need these weapons; I do not wish to be protected by these weapons of wholesale destruction. "I am in my Lord's hand, and there I will remain." "Nothing can happen to me but what he has provided, and what is for my salvation." With this resolve, which must convert our inmost thoughts, and turn them into the way of peace, faith gains vital reality. Such groups of believers can then spread a spirit of true reason, peace-loving reason, in their nations. "I wish to live without armament" – with this personal resolve for my personal life it begins. Since always, in all world-transformation and world-improvement, we must begin with ourselves. "To create peace without arms" that is then the political way in which I would like to influence my environment, my people, for which I agitate with all like-minded people, and seek to persuade others. So Jesus' way goes, from a personal way of life, and becomes a spirit of repentance for all peoples. If on a Day of National Remembrance, a man asks whether there are not better ways than the old ways, we point him to Jesus, Joseph's son, and if he has his doubts whether any help is to be found in that quarter, then the best that we can say to him is – better than all attempts to prove our case – "Come and see, and put the way of this Jesus to the test!"

Christmas

A friend has asked me to write for a newspaper under his direction an exposition of the last part of John 3 suitable for Christmas. I ask you now to be willing for such an external reason to deal with this text today. This example shows how artificial is our division of the course of the year into the seasons of the Ecclesiastical Year. This means that we divide up the content of the Gospel according to seasons. At Christmas we think of the Incarnation of God, on Good Friday we sorrow under the Cross, at Easter we rejoice over the Resurrection, and finally, at Pentecost we remember the Holy Spirit. And yet all these things are inseparable and every time, on every Sunday we ought to be thinking of the whole, the Gospel always speaks of the whole thing together, of Easter, of Christmas, and of Pentecost. So now let us hear a text which is intended for a Christmas exposition.

He who comes from above is above all, he who is of the earth belongs to the earth, and of the earth he speaks; he who comes from heaven is above all. He bears witness to what he has seen and heard, yet no one receives his testimony; he who receives his testimony sets his seal to this, that God is true. For he whom God has sent utters the words of God, for it is not by measure that he gives the Spirit; the Father loves the Son, and has given all things into his hand. He who believes in the Son has eternal life; he who does not obey the Son shall not see life, but the wrath of God rests on him. John 3, 31–36.

That is Christmas, clothed in difficult words. Nothing about Bethlehem, manger, shepherds, very abstract words. The key-words of the whole Gospel of John are gathered together in a *resumé.* As often on other occasions, the Johannine Evangelist seems quite cut off from our practical life, from politics and society, quite absorbed in the mystery of Jesus, so that our world seems absolutely lost to him. But if one reflects in detail on his sentences, as we are now going to do together, one notices that even he is doing nothing but tell a story, a story of this world of ours, in which the whole of our reality is contained.

We can, however, notice this at once when we hear that he is speaking of the earth, of our earth. *"He who is of the earth belongs to the earth, and of the earth he speaks."* That is the most modern sentence in the Bible, the final result of a long history of the spirit; man a late product of millions of years of the earth's development, a highly developed, perhaps also very perverted animal, an earthly, sensuous, physical, transitory being, which here wages its struggle for existence, and one day with this earth will also perish, dreaming of higher things, but never raising itself above earthly things. Materialism is the final truth about man, and idealism, the idea that man comes from above, from the Spirit, and not from below, from matter, is a self-deception which must be overcome. That is the modern world-view. It has the whole of science to speak for it.

Here, in this text, there is certainly talk of an "above". If one reads superficially, this does not seem to give us any help. *"He who comes from above is above all."* That is evident and clear. He who is above can trample on those who are below. The man who stands erect is better placed than the man who lies on the ground. The man who can fly in the sky can drop bombs on houses below. The man who can first set up an observation station on the moon, can dominate the whole world. The man who has the upper hand is above everyone else. In addition to this men have conceived of a still higher altitude, a divine altitude, of gods who stand wholly above us and are more powerful than men. These gods have often enough also served to legitimate those who ranked high in human society, in order that the underdogs, the subjects, should acknowledge them, and every revolt against those above should from the start be hopeless as well as reprehensible. In so far materialism is a movement of liberation, because here those who are below are saying to those above, "You too are only of the earth, your position above us has only earthly justification, no heavenly justification, and you may deck yourselves out as much as you please with divine authority, we shall still pull you down from your exalted height". *"What is of the earth is earthly",* and is therefore equal, and no one has a divine claim higher than another.

On a superficial reading it appears as if our text also were involved in the protest against the religious glorification of those above in society in order that they may be able to keep down those who are below. But what is written here is not, "He who is above is over all". What is written is "He who *comes* from above is over all". What is spoken of here is a coming. Of whose coming, of whom does the Evangelist speak? We know this; he speaks of Jesus. What did Jesus' coming look like? He came, as the Apostle Paul says, in Philippians 2, he did not remain above, did not count his superiority a thing to be grasped at, but came down into human existence, into a slave-existence, to a place where he was spat upon, trodden down, and put to death. Thus anyone who wishes to find the "above" of which the whole Bible speaks, must, strange though it may seem, go right down below here on earth. The paradox is that what is of the earth, the thought that is of earthly origin, is actually a striving upwards, everyone wants to get on top; while on the contrary what is here called the true divine "above", is a striving downwards, and is only to be found at the lowest point of the earth, on the gallows among the most downtrodden and outcast of society, with one who has no longer a place in it, in the grave which is the destiny of us all. There in the depths the Lord of glory of the religions is not to be found, but the servant God of the Gospel, the ministering, self-sacrificing brother Jesus who "and no other one" is the living Lord of the Gospel.

This implies a change, indeed a double change in our earthly life-situation for us earthly men, who are of the earth. The one thing is, that at the first glance there seem to stand here two closed circles over against each other, hopelessly separated from one another. Here is the realm of the earthly. No one can transcend it. To put it philosophically for some of us, the Bible does not believe in idealistic transcendence. Man, as an earthworm, dust from dust, cannot raise himself from the earth, cannot climb into the divine sphere. What is of the earth, is of the earth.

And here is the other circle, the circle of the divine life. If the earth is the world in which man strangles and devours man, and in which we all incur guilt, the world of altogether limited, narrow love and great lovelessness, the divine life is the life of the great eternal love and blessedness. The Gospel of John sees the two circles as hopelessly separated from each other. "That which is born of the flesh is flesh, and that which is born of the Spirit is spirit", he says in the same chapter (3, 6), and in another place, "You are from below, I am from above" (8, 23). The Jesus event, disclosed to men whose eyes have been opened, the eyes of the first community, and the eyes of those among them who as their spokesmen have written for us the New Testament, the Jesus event is the removal of the separation of these two circles. The coming of Jesus is the bond, the event of descending love, is the appearing of new life, of life undreamt of, of eternal life in the earthly life. *"The Father loves the Son"; it says here, "And has given everything into his hands."* The whole of divine life here below, and man, the poor earthworm, earthly life here below, and men the poor earthworms *no longer alone,* no more the prey of transitoriness, and guilt, no longer devouring each other, new possibilities in the midst of the old earth.

But their presence is of such a kind that here on earth the old antithesis between these two spheres, the earthly and the divine, repeats itself once more. There are two quite sharp antitheses standing side by side in our text. On the one hand we are told *"He who is of the earth, speaks of the earth"* and then on the other hand there is the sentence *"He whom God has sent utters the words of God"*. On the one hand we are told *"yet no one receives his testimony",* and then at once the next words *"He who receives his testimony sets his seal to this, that God is true".* What kind of contrasts are these? First there is the one contrast; the new Word and all men, we who come from the earth; Jesus and all of us, he from above – we from the earth. Jesus, the new possibility and reality of God, is an impossibility on earth, and to which of you, when words of the Gospel really touch him through the wall of custom, is not their impossibility at once evident? How impossible we shall at once notice. Jesus, with his different nature, with his tendency downwards, with his love and his call to follow him in love, stands as an alien over against the earthly, that which is of the earth.

Granted, externally here everything seems equally earthly. The people speaking here are all earthly. Even this Jesus is one of them. One does not see anything external in him to show that he comes "from above". There is no direct voice speaking down from heaven. They are all merely men, even this Jesus of Nazareth, also his disciples, and those who kill him, all merely men and human words. But between the human words there arises a violent contrast. The one group continue to sing the old song, religious or philosophical, stupid or clever, godless or religious, theistic or atheistic, the old song of the earth. The others have heard something new, they strike up a new song, a new message of new life, new love, of new men, of a new God. But the new has no prospect of success on earth.

Against this hopelessness there stands here a hopeful word: *"It is not by measure that he gives the Spirit"*, not meagrely measured out, not so that only Jesus gets something from it, while everyone else goes empty away. The Spirit – that is the penetrating dynamic of Jesus. Jesus as dynamite. That is the power of the Gospel. It is promised that nothing can resist it; that it embeds itself like a goad, that it makes us a battle-field between the earthly and that which comes from above, that it wills something from us that we are unwilling to do, and in spite of this brings us to do it, – gives us something that we had never desired enough. It makes that possible which before was impossible, it gives fulfilment undreamt of, it can overcome the fear of death, it can free our mouth, it can open our ears, give sight to our eyes. That can happen, and only because it has repeatedly happened, is there a Christian Church today, a Christian fellowship in spite of all the misuse of the Gospel in the Church.

If the Gospel has penetrated to us, then things happen which stand here side by side: *"No one receives his testimony; but he who receives his testimony . . ."* Just as at the beginning of John's Gospel "His own people received him not, but to all who received him" . . . (John 1, 11f.) Suddenly there are deserters from the camp of the earthly to the camp of the divine, the divine has come down to us, and they *"seal it"*. That is a splendid word. As Martin Luther King went in front of his scavengers, and knew that that could at any moment happen which indeed happened, he set his seal that *"God is true"*. As Dietrich Bonhoeffer joined the conspiracy, and knew that it could cost him his head, he set his seal to this, that *"God is true"*. As Camillo Torres went into the mountains to the guerillas, in order to bring his people to self-awareness, and knew that this would be his death, he set his seal to this. When thousands of young men in America prefer to go to prison rather than share the murder in Vietnam, then they set their seal to this. To what do they set their seal? What does it mean, that God is true? It means that the way of God is the true one. What way of God? The way downwards from privileges to the service of sacrificial love.

The central problem today, more clearly recognized by the young people than by our Church traditions, is at the same time the central problem of the New Testament; what are we doing with our privileges? And what is God doing with his privileges? Every one of us, in contrast with someone, probably in contrast with many people, is a privileged person. I can think three clear thoughts in sequence, and am very privileged in contrast with mentally retarded people who cannot do that; I can see, and am privileged in contrast with the blind; I have good qualities, people like me, and so I am privileged in contrast with a person who shows outwardly only his bad qualities, and whom nobody likes; I have a wholesome self-esteem, and am privileged in contrast with someone who is distressed by his inferiority complex, which continually incite him to wrong behaviour. What am I doing with my privileges? That is just as true of the whole of society's propertied classes bristling with arms, propertied nations bristling with arms today, and we Christians belong to the rich and satiated third of mankind. By means of religion and soldiers and laws the privileges are defended. The whole system of society is built up on privilege, and is there to defend the privileges of society. What are we doing with our privileges, which none of us is so ready seriously to renounce. Who will free us from our servitude to our privileges? Who will free us for discipleship, for imitation of God? For he is the one who does not hold on to his privileges, who did not remain on the throne of Lordship, but spent himself and gave himself to sinners, to the men of privilege, to free them from enslavement to their privileges.

Now, friends, the last verse is pointed at us. *"He who believes in the Son has eternal life, he who does not obey the Son shall not see life, but the wrath of God rests on him."* Here it becomes clear; the wrath of God is not the grim verdict of punishment uttered by an angry despot at some Last Judgement still afar off, it is the present judgement upon our bondage to our privileges, coming from the God who has shown to us by his example, what we ought to do with privileges. On this world there lies the wrath of God, on this rich white race of mankind there lies the wrath of God, on this America that pens a minority of people in slums, there lies, as we see today the wrath of God. Today we can clearly recognize that. When we do with privileges, what earthly thinking requires of us, then nothing else will be the harvest. Possessions, possessions, possessions, ever more possessions, and increasingly meaninglessness of life, ever more satiety, ever more clinics and psychiatric cases, ever more hostility and loneliness. The Gospel believes that it would heal our life if, in imitation of God we were to put our privileges both individually and collectively at the disposal of the underprivileged around us. In this manner we would see the life that just escapes us when we think earthly thoughts, when instead of going downwards, we strive upwards, and believe that thus we are gaining life. *"He who does not obey the Son shall not see life, but he who believes in the Son, will have eternal life."* To believe means: following on the way of the Son, who gave up his privileges, to build upon this, that God is true, that this is the true way to life, whatever it may cost us. He who thus from above comes down to us into the depths, he is the true Lord, he is above all, he shows us what is profitable and what is life indeed, he speaks and is the final truth.

You say that to us, Lord Jesus, that we may venture to take your way with you, and we ask you, help us to believe and to follow you obediently on your way, and show to us and advise us what that means every day.

Therefore-But

*Now about that time Herod the king stretched forth his hands to vex
certain of the Church. And he killed James the brother of John with the
sword. And because he saw it pleased the Jews, he proceeded further to
take Peter also. (Then were the days of unleavened bread.) And when he
had apprehended him, he put him in prison and delivered him to four
quaternions of soldiers to keep him, intending after Easter to bring him
forth to the people. Peter therefore was kept in prison; but prayer was
made without ceasing of the church unto God for him. And when Herod
would have brought him forth, the same night Peter was sleeping between two soliders, bound with two chains, and the keepers before the
door kept the prison. And, behold, the angel of the Lord came upon
him, and a light shined in the prison; and he smote Peter on the side, and
raised him up, saying Arise up quickly. And his chains fell off from his
hands. And the angel said unto him, Gird thyself, and bind on thy
sandals. And so he did. And he saith unto him, Cast thy garment about
thee, and follow me. And he went out, and followed him; and wist not
that it was true which was done by the angel; but thought he saw a vision.
When they were past the first and second ward, they came unto the iron
gate which leadeth unto the city; which opened to them of his own
accord; and they went out, and passed on through one street; and
forthwith the angel departed from him. And when Peter was come to
himself, he said Now I know of a surety, that the Lord hath sent his
angel, and hath delivered me out of the hand of Herod, and from all the
expectation of the people of the Jews. And when he had considered the
thing, he came to the house of Mary the mother of John, whose surname
was Mark; where many were gathered together praying. And as Peter
knocked at the door of the gate, a damsel came to hearken, named
Rhoda. And when she knew Peter's voice, she opened not the gate for
gladness, but ran in, and told how Peter stood before the gate. And they
said unto her. Thou art mad. But she constantly affirmed that it was even
so. Then said they, It is his angel. But Peter continued knocking: and
when they had opened the door, and saw him, they were astonished. But
he, beckoning unto them with the hand to hold their peace, declared unto
them how the Lord had brought him out of the prison. And he said, Go,
shew these things unto James, and to the brethren. And he departed, and
went into another place.* Acts 12, 1–17.

In the old version which I have just read, this story sounds very
edifying, a little bit like a beautiful old fairy story. But it sounds very
different in the language of our day, turned into journalese. So I am
going to read it now like a report in a modern newspaper – the Sunday
Express. (Of course in a well-ordered Jewish town there are no Sunday
newspapers, because people there still know that the gift of one day of
rest should not be disgraced as it is with us, but let us disregard that for
the moment, so the Sunday Express, with great headlines:

Mysterious liberation of prisoner in Jerusalem!
Flight of Terrorist!
Legal Authorities investigate prison scandal.
"Last night a Galilean prisoner Simon Jonasson, who in his circle has
the nickname Petros (Rocky), under arrest in Jerusalem prison on
suspicion of membership of a criminal gang, was in a manner still
unexplained set free, probably by members of his gang. Although
special security measures had been taken, his accomplices have clearly
succeeded in making imitation keys and drugging the watch. The
escaped man is a member of the hard core of the so-called Galilean
Gang whose leader Jesus of Nazareth was apprehended fourteen years
ago through the co-operation of our authorities with the Occupying
Power and executed. On that occasion Simon, the man who has now
escaped, attempted to prevent by violence the arrest of Jesus, and
inflicted a severe head wound on a police official, cutting off his ear.
The gang, which confined itself to agitation hostile to the State, but had
cross-connections with the Zealot Guerillas in the Jewish mountains,
of whom two were executed with the aforesaid Jesus, was at first
broken up by the liquidation of its leader, and the remaining members
went underground, but reassembled themselves and in recent days
have been thrusting themselves more and more impudently before the
notice of the public. They created a commune on a communist basis,
and won sympathizers by the assertion that their leader Jesus was still
alive, or had returned to life. They claimed that he would soon change
the whole world, and set up a Communist kingdom in the place of all
present Governments. Our authorities, who rightly saw in this agitation a danger for our social order, and for the peaceful relationship
between the Occupying Power and our State, have for some time been
observing the activities of the gang, and have now struck. One of the
ringleaders, a certain James, was executed, others, among them
Simon, were arrested and submitted to a thorough investigation. It is to
be feared that today's liberation of the prisoner will give a fresh
impetus to the gang. Its provocations can lead to reactions on the part
of the Occupying Power, whose consequences would have to be borne
by the whole population. For this reason it is only to be hoped that the
activities of these messianic utopians, who have lost all sense of reality,
and have become a public danger, will as quickly as possible be brought
to an end. The Legal Authorities have at once begun an investigation
of this scandal at the prison, and will certainly see to it that the guilty
officials, who have already been put under arrest, are made to answer
for their misdemeanour. The hunt for the escaped man, who has gone
underground, is already in full cry."
    So far the "Sunday Express". Note however, such translation into
the language of a modern newspaper does not mean that the terrorists
of today are set on a level with Jesus, but this does make it clear that
Jesus – crucified between two guerillas, under the accusation of being
one himself – and this first band of his followers were equated by the
Jewish and Roman authorities of that day with a terrorist criminal

association. And if this was a calumny, yet this was only possible, because there were indications of such a thing, to which an appeal could be made. After all, this Jesus had come forward with a Messianic claim, and had announced the imminent divine world-revolution.

In a Psalm in his honour which had been put in the mouth of his mother, it was stated that he would cast down the mighty from their thrones, and exalt the oppressed (Luke 1, 51). He himself had called Herod the King (who was his sovereign) a fox, and in his trial by the Governor Pilate, he had admitted, if in somewhat ambiguous language, that he claimed a king's throne; some people claimed to have heard from his own mouth that he would destroy and rebuild in three days the Temple, the shrine of the Jews, that even the Romans had not laid hands upon. Two of his followers were Zealot guerillas, (Simon the Zealot and Judas Iscariot (Luke 6, 15–16). A part of his company was armed (Luke 22, 38). And this Peter had, in fact, by intervening with the sword, tried violently to prevent the arrest of Jesus by the police. And what was said about the Commune on a Communist basis was not false (Acts 2, 44f, 4, 32–7).

There were indeed other words of this Jesus, in favour of non-violence, and of paying taxes, but his calumniators kept quiet about this, and it was not to be denied that this group too, with its Messianism, belonged to the environment of the contemporary groups who were disturbing the peace, and owing to the facts mentioned, stood in an ambiguous light. So it could be understandable if the authorities responsible for peace and order in the explosive situation did not carefully distinguish between violent and non-violent creators of unrest, but threw them all together into the same pot, and believed themselves compelled to proceed against them all with the same rigour. The fact that these were the beginnings of the Christian community, that from the beginning it was regarded as a very dangerous group for the State and the social order, what has that to say to us still at this present day for the relation between a true Christian fellowship and its environment? It can at some times be, as Luke has earlier recorded in the book of Acts (2, 47), that, because of its piety, because of its exemplary care of the poor, because of its social benevolence, the Community is popular with the rest of the populace. But it can happen that these sympathies swing round into violent enmity, and that the powerful in society, with the official representative of the State, with all the propaganda machine, declare war on the fellowship, with calumnies and half-truths, and this for the reason that the brotherly life of the fellowship, the abolition of all barriers of station, class, of sex and race, calls in question the whole of the rest of the social order, which is built up upon these barriers. By so doing the fellowship anticipates what it hopes for on the return of its eagerly awaited Lord; he will set up the Kingdom of God on earth, and in the Kingdom there will no longer be rich and poor, no longer master and servant, no longer privilege on the ground of the colour of one's skin, or of possessions, or of education, or the male sex, or special achievements, but only brotherly service of all for all. With this expectation of such a Kingdom of God, all the systems of privilege in which we live, together with the defence by all means of these privileges of the rich against the poor, the strong against the weak, the white against the coloured, are unmasked as being opposed to God's will. God is not willing to have that any longer, and therefore his people can no longer justify it in God's name, as the religions and churches have often done. The Advent Church's hope of the Kingdom of God inexorably uncovers the injustice in our social system. As an Advent Church it awaits the new Kingdom of the justice and brotherliness of God and of men. But as an Advent Church it does not wait in inactivity, but begins now in a preliminary manner and according to its limited powers; to do in its common life and in its external influence upon society what it can for the realization of human rights, for a life of man in society according to the will of God; that is what is meant by waiting for Advent, and when we do live in that manner, we have to expect difficult tensions, even conflicts, between a genuine Christian community and the existing society.

And now for another aspect of the significance of this story for us, linked with a memory. On Sunday, 5th July, 1937, five days after Martin Niemöller's arrest, we began in St. Anne's Church near here our services of intercession, for which members of the Confessing Church assembled daily for eight years. In this first service of intercession, I preached on a verse in the story we are considering. *"Therefore Peter was kept in prison, but prayer was made without ceasing unto God for him."*

This *Therefore – But* is the characteristic mark of the life of the Advent Church and all the disciples of Jesus in this world. Add together all the God-defying crimes in this world; arrest and torture and the death of those who fight against injustice and tyranny, all that fills the files of Amnesty International, add to this the world famine of today, the frequent collapse of the best efforts to change and improve conditions, and the frequent victory of wicked men, add to these the days of excessive anxiety in our personal life, the fears that beset us in hospital, and our mourning when our loved ones die – add all this together as the burden of the world – and then say Therefore – But! *Therefore* everything is thus, as it is, and it is bad that it is so. *But* that is never the whole story, *but* this world with its terrors is never alone, *but* this world, however much it tries, cannot escape from its Lord, who loves it; *but* he who sends his disciples into this world of wolves to serve this world of wolves is with them every day until the consummation; *but* he hears us, when no one else still hears us, even through the thickest prison walls. So we prefix this word, "That is the way the world is", with a 'therefore', and counter it with a 'but'; "the world is therefore as it is, but he is at our side, with his Spirit and his gifts" – but he hears us, when we cry to him.

The prayer in which we set this *but* over against the *therefore*, is itself a means of his help and strengthening. The Church was indeed then forced to go underground and could only assemble behind locked doors, and Peter was hardly set free before he had to go underground in order to escape the pursuit. No angel indeed rescued Martin Niemöller, who is among us today, from the concentration camp in which he was held prisoner for eight years of his life. But the fact that we were permitted and able to interpose the *but* of prayer, he inside the prison, and we outside of it, helped us immeasurably in those dark days of tyranny and war, and made us able to resist the temptations of the Regime, and the temptation of hopelessness and despair.

In those days, when this story of the wonderful liberation of Peter was told, written down, and passed round the churches, the persecution had already spread. Then and there came arrests and torture and executions, and Peter himself had to die in Rome a martyr's death on the cross, and no angel from heaven came and opened yet again the prison doors. How then, in spite of this, did this story bring them consolation and strength? The Bible calls the individual visible acts of God's help *"Signs"*. They passed on this story as a sign, not as a guarantee that things would turn out as wonderfully for every imprisoned witness to Jesus Christ, only as a sign – a sign of what?

The story is in the first place a sign of the infinite possibilities to help us of him to whom we call, more than our imagination can think of, and certainly much more than is possible for our fear to conceive of. The story here sounds to us like a beautiful legend, and none of us counts upon an angel from heaven. But "God's angels have no wings" is the title of a fine book by Claus Westermann, the Old Testament Professor at Heidelberg, about the angels in the Bible. God's messengers (for "angel" really means messenger!) do not necessarily have the sheen of the angels on the Christmas Tree, God can send help, strength and salvation by commonplace and very earthly messengers, and if we are alert, and look at things in this way, then we must allow that God has already sent many angels into our life, to help us inwardly and outwardly.

Second: the story is a sign, but not a guarantee of salvation. Many were saved from the utmost danger in astonishing, very wonderful ways, many were not saved, but put to death in spite of all prayers. "Our God is *able* to deliver us from the burning fiery furnace" said Daniel (3, 17) but he is not compelled to do so, and one day Peter must die, all people saved from death must die. Then it will sometimes appear to us, as if we had on the contrary to say "We indeed pray without ceasing, but those for whom we pray still remain in their outward and inward prisons of distress". No, it is precisely to prevent this that the sign of the liberation of Peter is meant. It says to Peter, to the Church of that day, and to us all, that he who speaks to us, who loves us, who sends us into the world to our fellow men, who ever and again gives us single visible indications of his help, stays by us in every situation. No hair can fall from our heads without his will, and when he permits not only one hair, but our whole head to fall, and when someone is not saved, but perishes in the persecution, in spite of all, the bond between him and us is not broken. "No one can take you out of my hand." (John 10, 29.) With this promise he invites us to trust him for the dangerous way of his discipleship, and in this trust we set one thing against the other. It is *indeed* as it is, *but* we do not cease to call on him, to trust him, to wait upon him.

The Great Disturbance

*About that time there arose no little stir concerning the Way. For a man
named Demetrius, a silversmith, who made silver shrines of Artemis,
brought no little business to the craftsmen. These he gathered together,
with the workmen of like occupation, and said, "Men, you know that
from this business we have our wealth. And you see and hear that not
only at Ephesus but almost throughout all Asia this Paul has persuaded
and turned away a considerable company of people, saying that gods
made with hands are no gods. And there is danger that not only this trade
of ours may come into disrepute but also that the temple of the great
goddess Artemis may count for nothing, and that she may even be
deposed from her magnificence, she whom all Asia and the world
worship."*

*When they heard this they were enraged and cried out "Great is
Artemis of the Ephesians!" So the city was filled with the confusion, and
they rushed together into the theatre, dragging with them Gaius and
Aristarchus, Macedonians who were Paul's companions in travel. Paul
wished to go in among the crowd, but the disciples would not let him;
some of the Asiarchs also, who were friends of his, sent to him and
begged him not to venture into the theatre. Now some cried one thing,
some another, for the assembly was in confusion, and most of them did
not know why they had come together. Some of the crowd prompted
Alexander, whom the Jews had put forward. And Alexander motioned
with his hand, wishing to make a defence to the people. But when they
recognized that he was a Jew, for about two hours they all with one voice
cried out, "Great is Artemis of the Ephesians!" And when the town clerk
had quieted the crowd, he said, "Men of Ephesus, what man is there who
does not know that the city of the Ephesians is temple keeper of the great
Artemis, and of the sacred stone that fell from the sky? Seeing then that
these things cannot be contradicted, you ought to be quiet and do
nothing rash. For you have brought these men here who are neither
sacrilegious nor blasphemers of our goddess. If therefore Demetrius and
the craftsmen with him have a complaint against any one, the courts are
open and there are proconsuls; let them bring charges against one
another. But if you seek anything further, it shall be settled in the regular
assembly. For we are in danger of being charged with rioting today,
there being no cause that we can give to justify this commotion." And
when he had said this, he dismissed the assembly.* Acts 19, 23–20, 1.

This is another crazy story. How lively and colourful is Luke's account,
and how up to date! Demetrius has made the discovery that the Gospel
is bad for business, and the Gospel endangers the level of employment.
His business books, his reduced turnover shows it to him. Since this
Paul-agitation is spreading, and an ever-increasing number of people
who were hitherto loyal worshippers of the gods are turning to this
Jewish sect of Christ-worshippers, the demand is dropping for the

beautiful little silver temples which are produced by the home-labour of many craftsmen, and which he as wholesale dealer in religious trinkets has been accustomed to sell to the thousands of pilgrims who come on pilgrimage to the world-famous temple of Artemis (Diana) in Ephesus. Everyone has at home a small model of the Temple standing on his desk. Demetrius mobilizes the whole town, "It is not only my business that is at stake, we are all in the same boat! What will come of Ephesus if this kind of atheism, this contempt of the gods spreads, and our great shrine no longer counts for anything? Can these people be allowed to desecrate our holiest things, and say that what is made by hands is of no importance? And not only our level of employment, our whole order of society is in danger, since it is built on the basis of religion. And who can guarantee to us that the gods are really power-less as this little carpet-bagging Jew and carpet maker claims? Perhaps there really is something in religion, and these gods will in anger revenge themselves on the town of Ephesus because of the spread of this neglect!"

We could from our modern standpoint say to a man with such concerns, "Friend Demetrius, the time of heathenism is now irretriev-ably past! If you intend to keep up your profits and the number of your employees, you must change to a product that is not hostile to the will of the true, living God, that is not hostile to the Gospel to which the peoples are now turning." "Which?" he will ask, and if we are to give him advice, we are all at once involved in the difficult questions of economics and politics. Perhaps he suggests to us that he should now turn to the production of armaments, perhaps start up a business for the delivery of arms, today a fairly safe job, e.g. in the very modern production of neutron bombs, or perhaps he should change over to the business of atomic power. Then he will hear how these things are very much a subject of debate among Christians. In order to be safe, in the end, instead of the manufacture of devotional trinkets he opens a business for importing tropical fruits. But there too, people come to him and say "Not only what is produced, but the manner of production can be against the Gospel, and the man who buys bananas produced by the United Fruit Company or Californian grapes or iceberg salad or South African Uitspan Oranges makes himself an accomplice in the inhuman exploitation of the plantation workers in these countries."

We get into some embarrassment when we allow the Gospel to have something to say in questions of Economics. It is necessary to inform ourselves, often enough we do not know who is right, often enough too, we do not know what we can take part in professionally or commercially without injury to our conscience. As our story shows, if we take the Gospel seriously in the practice of our life, we come unexpectedly into conflict with powerful interests. The representatives of these interests then act mostly as Demetrius did, they argue not only about their own profits, but more on social lines, about providing employment for others, for the poor, and above all, with religion.

When Kaiser Wilhelm II seventy years ago warned about the

"yellow peril", "Nations of Europe, defend your most sacred things!": everything was confused here, the Gospel, the great colonial enterprise, and the political power of the German Empire, and so here with Demetrius: "Citizens of Ephesus, defend your most sacred things, and also your level of employment and my profits!"

The conclusion for us today, drawn from this example from the beginnings of the Christian Church:

1. Collisions with interests, even with powerful interests, cannot be avoided. The Book of Acts tells of a whole series of such collisions. It is not great peace which expands on all sides nor joyful agreement that resounds when the Gospel is proclaimed, it is rather conflict which arises on every hand. Everyone who is apprehended by this message moves into a deeply disquieted life. He can no longer take part in things in which he previously took part; he comes into conflict with himself, with his previous thinking and willing, and also into all kinds of conflict with his environment. "I am not come" says Jesus the bringer of peace, and Prince of peace, "to bring peace, but a sword. For I am come to set a man against his father, and the daughter against her mother, and the daughter-in-law against her mother-in-law, and a man's enemies will be those of his own household." (Matthew 10, 34–36.)

The Gospel does indeed give us important guidance and help *how* we are to decide conflicts in a new, no longer murderous manner, and therefore it is really a message of peace. But it leaves us in no doubt that it is leading not into a harmonious, peaceful life, but a life full of conflicts "fighting without, fear within" (2 Cor. 7, 5) as Paul once confesses of himself. Where the Church and its environment live only in harmony without conflict, one must be suspicious. It could be that this is a peace which has been brought at the price of an abbreviation and misrepresentation of the Gospel.

2. The Gospel's purpose is to make us very wary when these three things, the sacred, the level of employment and profit are brought together. It makes us mistrustful of a mixture in which appeal made to the most sacred values serves only to maintain very material interests.

3. Its purpose is to set us free to become critical of inhumanity in our own society, and to work for a better society in which the God-given powers of men are not cast on the ash-heap of unemployment, and are not used to increase employment where the work serves death, and the poisoning of the earth instead of for life.

But the thrust of the Gospel does not only disturb the business concerns of the big entrepreneur Demetrius, it also disturbs the peace of religious people. This shows itself in the case of another figure in our story, the Jew Alexander. His appearance is to be explained in this way; the Jewish community were in a precarious situation. There was anti-Semitism even in these days. In Ephesus they had every reason to lie low. For in that city many people made a livelihood from the tourist trade connected with the Temple of Diana. Its priests were, as a modern commentator (Ernst Haenchen) says, "at the same time a great Bank with far-spreading relations, and exercized the power of big capital". So it was important for the Jewish community that their Jewish faith in the God of Israel, and their disbelief in the "great majesty" of the goddess Artemis should not be regarded as an attack on the religion and business and social order of their environment.

Now comes this Jew Paul, and by bringing the faith in the one God of Israel to the Gentile world also, disturbs the equilibrium of this tolerance. We Jews have our God, you Gentiles have your gods, we don't interfere with you, and you don't interfere with us; let everyone be saved in his own manner. The Ephesians take this new Christian community of Jews and non-Jews to be a Jewish sect. They will begin to think that "now the Jews are starting to make an attack on our religion and social order, and we must retaliate on them for that!" Now some of the crowd drag forward the Jew Alexander – probably a leading man in the local synagogue, whom they have recognized – in order to accuse him, and he prepares himself to make a speech in defence – not, of course a speech in defence of Paul and the Christian community, but a speech of defence about the harmlessness of the Jews. But the raging mob of people will not even give him a hearing, for them one Jew is as good as another, and they shout him down with their ritual choral shout *"Great is Diana of the Ephesians"*.

What can we learn from that? At that time the Jews repudiated and worked against this new group of adherents to Jesus to save their own skins, and, later, for centuries the Christians in a highly un-Christian manner oppressed and persecuted the Jews. That is a story with its own significance, certainly one that does us Christians no credit. But at that time Jews and Christians belonged together – at least in this respect, which was the issue in the great tumult in Ephesus; neither of them had any faith in these gods, both of them placed all their faith in the God of Israel. The Confession of both of them was what Demetrius here – in words of the biblical Prophets! – denounces as the blasphemous teaching of Paul *"that gods made with hands are not gods"* (v. 26). Both together must take responsibility for this fall of the gods, and be ready to suffer for it. But now, for the sake of its peace, the Jewish community does not take sides with this Christ-group, with Paul, but distances itself from them, and by so doing, from its own Confession. Alexander with his Jewish community represents here something that we in the Church have repeatedly experienced, both in the Church struggle and now everywhere in the world where the Gospel is proclaimed aggressively against the servitude of men under deified powers, and against the admixture of religion and profit. They represent the part of God's people that wishes to be left in peace, that has withdrawn itself into its tolerated corner, and wishes to avoid the conflicts into which the Gospel brings us. But the Gospel is the attack on the things that enslave us, and on all enslaving powers, and a Gospel that no longer attacks is no longer a message of joy and freedom for all men, for the others also around us, but is transformed into a religion of egoism, faith in a corner, which is concerned only for its own salvation.

Now let us look at the third figure in this story, at the man who was the cause of all this confusion, Paul. He does not come on the scene at all; he sits in concealment in a house, surrounded by his own people, the newly-won associates in the faith, who urge on him that he has already sufficiently exposed himself, and should not lay himself open to the hatred of the infuriated crowd. Then from another side the crowd is challenged by the representatives of the State authority to take the regular legal steps and not provoke by tumult the intervention of the police, and when in consequence things have quieted down, Paul leaves the town, in order to continue elsewhere his missionary work.

This does not impress us, for it does not look very heroic. And yet, it is just in this point that it is instructive for us, not in order to defend Paul under all circumstances, but in order to do him justice, and thereby to learn from him. Of both Jesus and of Paul we hear that at times they concealed themselves and withdrew themselves from danger. That means, in the first place, that *in* danger, *in* persecution, we should stand up like men and women, and pray for power and courage to make our confession. That is God's command. But it is not the command of God to be an adventurer, to seek out danger for its own sake, to thrust ourselves madly and rashly into persecution, or to provoke it. He is not a coward who withdraws from persecution, where it is possible to do so without betrayal. He is a coward who through betrayal, through keeping silent and omitting to do and say what he ought, avoids persecution, and he too, who keeps aloof from the persecuted and thereby betrays his own cause.

And, secondly; there are two kinds of provocation: provocation through our bearing, and behaviour, and provocation for the cause. Paul did not shrink from provocation for the cause. He called men away from the powers that enslaved them, to freedom given by the love of the living God. This provocation he implanted and anchored in the town of Ephesus by gathering together the congregation in that place. This provocation will remain, even if he goes. For this cause he here and in many places risked his life, and brought upon himself grievous maltreatment, which was at the end to lead to his martyrdom. If he had not now permitted his comrades to restrain him, if he had gone to this wild popular concourse, he would have been shouted down like Alexander, perhaps would also have been lynched. Then the Gospel would have lost him, the Apostle who bore it from one town to another, but the Gospel would have won nothing by this provocation. That is one rational consideration and an example that goes to prove that the command to bear witness and to confess our faith does not exclude, but takes into account, rational considerations. We must not be blind, but reasonable witnesses, we must not shun conflicts, but we must not provoke them either by unreflecting behaviour or even by intention. It must be the cause itself which is committed to us, which provokes the conflict, and only then will it appear whether it is an inevitable, necessary conflict, or one that we could have, and should have, avoided.

The criterion will always be that of love. Do we wish through the message of Christ to help people, or to offend them? If we wish to help them, then we shall tell it to them lovingly, and lovingly do what the message commands us, and avoid offence and conflict so long as it can be done without betrayal. Our wish will be to deliver people from guilt and suffering, not to heap additional guilt upon them.

Therefore let us pray to the Lord, who sends us into the world, for courage, readiness to suffer, to stand firm and confident, and to take bold risks – asking at the same time for quiet, love, skill and judgement, all in service of the fair task of the Gospel, the message of joy, freedom, and peace.

Words of Farewell to Ensure Continuance

And from Miletus Paul sent to Ephesus and called to him the elders of the Church. And when they came to him, he said to them: You yourselves know how I lived among you all the time from the first day that I set foot in Asia, serving the Lord with all humility and with tears and with trials which befell me through the plots of the Jews; how I did not shrink from declaring to you anything that was profitable, and teaching you in public and from house to house, testifying both to Jews and to Greeks of repentance to God and of faith in our Lord Jesus Christ. And now, behold, I am going to Jerusalem, bound in the Spirit, not knowing what shall befall me there, except that the Holy Spirit testifies to me in every city that imprisonment and afflictions await me. But I do not account my life of any value nor as precious to myself, if only I may accomplish my course and the ministry which I received from the Lord Jesus, to testify to the gospel of the grace of God. And now, behold, I know that all you among whom I have gone about preaching the kingdom will see my face no more. Therefore I testify to you this day that I am innocent of the blood of all of you, for I did not shrink from declaring to you the whole counsel of God. Take heed to yourselves and to all the flock, in which the Holy Spirit has made you guardians, to feed the church of the Lord which he obtained with his own blood. I know that after my departure fierce wolves will come in among you, not sparing the flock; and from among your own selves will arise men speaking perverse things to draw away the disciples after them. Therefore be alert, remembering that for three years I did not cease night or day to admonish every one with tears. And now I commend you to God and to the word of his grace, which is able to build you up and to give you the inheritance among all those who are sanctified. I coveted no one's silver or gold or apparel. You yourselves know that these hands ministered to my necessities, and to those who were with me. In all things I have shown you that by so toiling one must help the weak, remembering the words of the Lord Jesus, how he said "It is more blessed to give than to receive".

And when he had spoken thus, he knelt down and prayed with them all. And they all wept and embraced Paul and kissed him, sorrowing most of all because of the word he had spoken, that they should see him no more. And they brought him to the ship. Acts 20, 17–36.

This is the last word of a last farewell. *"You all will see my face no more"* (v. 25). We all listen with strained attention to the last words of a person whom we love as if his whole life were summed up in them. We ask those who were present at his death, "What were his last words?", and are troubled when the last whisper was unintelligible, or when a person has been unable to say anything. But when in full consciousness someone has been able to write a farewell letter, then that is his most important bequest to us. Twenty-five years ago two friends and I published a volume with such letters of farewell that had

been written by people who had been put to death in Hitler's time
because of their loyalty to their faith, or their political responsibility.
("Du hast mich heimgesucht bei Nacht", published by H. Gollwitzer,
Käthe Kuhn, Reinhold Schneider; Gütersloher Taschenbücher n. 9.)
One sees from these letters how in face of death the spirit of the writer
concentrates itself, turning wholeheartedly to each of his dear ones to
whom he speaks for the last time, how he gathers together in a few
simple words what he has experienced and known to be the most
important things in life, and how as a result every word is filled with
immeasurable meaning.

In his account of the last missionary journey of the Apostle Paul,
Luke has now reached the day on which Paul takes farewell of his
congregations in order to go to Jerusalem. This time he makes this
decision, not on the basis of a rational calculation, such as we have
taken into consideration in his behaviour during the riot of Demetrius
a fortnight earlier, but now driven by a higher necessity, under an
imperative which stands peremptorily over him *"through the Spirit"*
(v. 23). It drives him irresistibly towards Jerusalem, the holy and
murderous city, "that kills the prophets, and stones those who were
sent to her" (Matthew 23, 37), to the city to which his Lord Jesus also
was drawn *"bound in the Spirit"* in order there to offer himself as a
sacrifice, in order to be put to death there. To this place Paul is also
being driven and drawn, and the same Spirit has said to him *"in every
city"* that *"imprisonment and afflictions await me there"* (v. 23). Luke
has of course no stenographer's notebook or manuscript of the
farewell words of the Apostle, he puts together everything that he
knows of Paul's preaching, and so now it is really a summarized
farewell message, concentrating upon what is most important in looking back on his life-work, and forwards to the future fortunes of this
work.

Paul is speaking to those who were the first that had been won for the
new life, and who now represent and lead the congregations which
have grown in number and size. When these congregations are here
called *"flocks"*, this should not disturb you as if this meant an inert or
stupid flock of sheep. These first Christian congregations were anything but a flock of sheep. Every individual Christian had, precisely
through the Gospel, become a very independent person, and was
compelled in his Gentile or Jewish environment to vindicate his new
life every day in an independent manner. Therefore the use of the
traditional expression "flock" at that time had nothing misleading or
belittling about it.

But every congregation must choose an order for itself, and in doing
so, appoint some people who take over special offices in service of this
order. Those who had responsibility for all the activities of the congregation, especially the arrangements and gatherings, were called
"Overseers", episkopoi, hence our word "Bishops". Our Presbyters,
the members of our Presbytery, are thus our Bishops. We must never
forget this, without thereby belittling our honoured Bishop Martin

Kruse in his special great responsibility. The fact that we have an episcopal leadership in our national Church, does not at all alter the fact that all Presbyters are Bishops, and that every congregation is called to be, not a flock of stupid imitative sheep, but a fellowship of responsible adult Christians.

Paul looks back on his work. This work was not the undertaking of a genius, a self-appointed leader and founder of a religion. It was *"a ministry that I received from the Lord Jesus"* (v. 24). What constituted this ministry? The ministry was a message *"the good news of the grace of God"* (v. 24). Its content is given by Paul in short concentrated formulae *"Repentance to God and faith in our Lord Jesus Christ"* (v. 21). *"The whole counsel of God"* (v. 27), or, as he says in one great word *"The Kingdom"* (v. 25). The Kingdom of God, proclaimed by the Prophets, incarnate in our midst in the coming of Jesus, the Messiah, our brother and Lord, the kingdom of life-bestowing grace for all men, that is "the whole will, the whole counsel of God", the new life that now seeks to spread itself abroad. This new life will and can transform old men, who live egoistically according to their own will, and by so doing destroy themselves and others, into men who live according to God's will, who have come from fear, loneliness and egoism to joy, hope, and a life for others, so that they spread around them an atmosphere of grace.

This ministry has brought to Paul *"tears and trials"* (v. 19), and it will again bring to him in Jerusalem *"imprisonment and afflictions"*, and in Rome, death. But this ministry was a joyful ministry. In it Paul has not remained solitary, but has won people for the same new life, who cling to him with tender love and gratitude, which shows itself by the fact that they are shaken and troubled by his announcement that they will not see him again, and say farewell to him with laments and kisses and tears.

But Paul not only feels the pain of this farewell. He is still more moved by looking forward to the future way of the congregation. He has no illusion that its life will be an idyll, protected by the watching care of God or received with approval, or at least tolerated in a liberal manner by the environment, or that it will be simply a triumphal progress. On the contrary! He knows that this congregation is under the protection of God – and at the same time threatened by the most severe dangers, and that from without as well as from within. *"I know that after my departure fierce wolves will come in among you, not sparing the flock, and from among your own selves will arise men speaking perverse things to draw away the disciples after them"* (v. 29f). You can imagine how relevant these words sounded to us in the Church struggle during the times of the Nazis, as they were literally fulfilled, the wild wolves of the Gestapo and the Party without, and in our very own midst the false doctrine of the German Christians, who held the Bishoprics, and seized power in the Church for themselves, and, almost worse, the many pastors and Church members who kept neutral, who came to terms with the enemy, who left the persecuted in their hour of need, in order to save their own skins. And as it was then with us, so now it is everywhere, where the new life demands public and active confession from us of faith and love, in the communist east, as in the so-called Christian and so-called free west. "Have no illusions" says Paul, "the protection of God will not fail you. But the protection of God does not protect you from outward persecution, nor yet from inner confusion. He protects you *in* the persecution and confusion. He helps you *in* the persecution to be upright and ready to suffer, and he helps you *in* the confusion to know what is true and what is false, and to distinguish between them." So faith is not a soft pillow on which we can rest. Faith is not to have sleep and rest, or to long for these things. In practice, faith means to trust in God's protection, and to watch against outward and inner danger, it means soberness instead of comforting illusions, it means to become critical, not to fall for everything that has a fine sound, not to hold that everything is Christian that gives itself out as Christian, and decks itself out in Christian language.

Paul says to these Bishops *"Take heed to yourselves and all the flock"* (v. 28). Here he certainly does not mean that they should do everything to protect the Church from confusion. This is the interpretation that we can sometimes hear today. It is said of all sorts of theological and political conceptions, that they should be kept far from the congregations, so that the congregations may not be confused. That is perhaps what must be done with a kindergarten, but not with a Christian congregation, for a Christian congregation is not a kindergarten. If it is, it is not a Christian congregation. The fact that such confusing conceptions arise is a consequence of the whole of our spiritual and social life, and also of the fact that our minds can be kept to the truth of the Gospel only by the Holy Spirit, and not through human compulsion. Once more; the Bishops must not protect the Church from confusion, but should help it, in confusion, to acknowledge the truth and to hold by the truth.

Nor does Paul in any way believe that the Bishops should set themselves up as the guarantors of the truth and pure doctrine, and compel the Church to follow them, just like a flock, in blind obedience, and then everything will go well. Paul says expressly, *"Take heed to yourselves"* for the men who *"say wrong things in order to draw away the disciples after them"*, can quite easily, as has often happened, be themselves Bishops, leading people in the Church. The right "taking heed" of a Bishop, a pastor, a Presbytery, will consist rather in penetrating ever anew and ever deeper into the truth of the Gospel, and consequently being not merely concerned with administrative tasks, but leading the fellowship to think for itself, to make its critical discoveries, and to distinguish between truth and falsehood, so that the fellowship may measure, judge, and call them to order – the Bishops, preachers, Presbyters and the leading members, by the standard of the Gospel. Every Christian must be a theologian. This was the case at that time, when the very seductive gnostic heresy in the time of early Christianity made such an impression upon the Christians. Had it not been recognized as false doctrine, and expelled, the Church would have been led away from the God of Israel and the crucified Jesus to all kinds of highly intellectual speculations and philosophies. If the dangers today seem quite different, yet the same watchfulness is necessary.

This does not indeed mean that today we should make all thinking in the Church uniform, and expel everyone who speaks of the Gospel in another than the old customary language, or who thinks he must draw from the Gospel other practical and political consequences than we do. The much lamented pluralism of the Church is not necessarily evil. It can also be a sign of Christian freedom. But in any case it is a challenge to us all to be continually distinguishing true from false, and helping each other to do so, and for this task we must arm ourselves by an ever deeper penetration into the Gospel, as God's witnesses, the Prophets and Apostles received it and handed it down to us.

What does a father or a mother do in the last farewell, looking forward anxiously on the further way of their beloved children? If they are well advised, two things.

1. They impart to their children as an inheritance what they themselves have acknowledged as right and true and pleasing to God, perhaps in writing, perhaps in a farewell letter, perhaps only in memory. Thus a tradition such as the Church passed on through the writings of the Prophets and Apostles. Such traditions are the human help which we can and should give to our successors, and as ourselves successors, we should not despise such traditions, but take from them what can be signposts to us for the present and the future.

2. All parents can, like the Apostle, know that their children, their successors have minds of their own, and must go their own way, and that they, the parents will no longer be able to lead and protect the children. Tradition is here an essential, but not sufficient help, and one can cite it, and one can put it aside, and one can also interpret it according to one's own understanding. Therefore well-advised parents, when they must leave their children, turn to him who is the true Father above all parents and children, and recommend their children to him, glad that they are allowed to do so, glad that God's power is promised to us where our power is at an end.

That is what Paul does here: *"Now I commend you to God and the word of his grace, which is able to build you up and to give you an inheritance among all those who are sanctified"* (v. 32). When we act thus, that reconciles us with the boundary which at the latest we reach at our death, with the boundary of our responsibilities, with the boundary of our solicitude for those who are dear to us. This boundary is a wholesome reminder to keep us humble; it is not we who rule the world, we do not even rule our children, nor do we rule the Church of Christ. With this humbling boundary we are reconciled by him who draws it for us. "Cast all your cares on me, *I* care for

you, for your children, for the Church, and for this whole poor
human race."

This is the last thing that Paul can do, that we all can do at this last
boundary. But it is not quite his final word. When in the case of a man
who has died, we ask "What was the very last thing he said?", then
perhaps in Paul's case we would expect an exhortation to hold fast to
the faith, or a word of thanks to Jesus. It is remarkable, however, that
Luke tells us as his last word of all, just like the last word that a dying
man, gathering together his last powers, breathes from his lips in order
to impart to us the quintessence of his life-experience: *"To give is more
blessed than to receive."*

Hope for the Hopeless

Therefore, since we are justified by faith, we have peace with God through our Lord Jesus Christ. Through him we have obtained access to this grace in which we stand, and we rejoice in our hope of sharing the glory of God. More than that, we rejoice in our sufferings, knowing that suffering produces endurance, and endurance produces character, and character produces hope, and hope does not disappoint us, because God's love has been poured into our hearts through the Holy Spirit which has been given to us. Romans 5, 1–6.

"Called to hope" – the motto for the Kirchentag of 1979, very much a live issue for every one of us, and by no means merely a pious Biblical formula. As someone at the University is called to a Professorship in order to take up an important position in University life, and to be a person who has something important to say, which is worth listening to, so have you Christians, the Jesus-group, received a call to take up an important position among men, to be people who exude hope. "It is only for the sake of the hopeless that hope is given to us" is an often-quoted word of Walter Benjamin, one of the profoundest thinkers of our century. Of course one must oneself have become a man with hope in order to be able to pass on hope to the hopeless. But hope is given to us to pass on, and not merely to have hope for ourselves, and let other people perish in their despair. Hope stands in contradiction to resignation. This contradiction goes right through us. It divides people today into the hopeful and the resigned, and it cuts in two our inner soul in the fight between hope and resignation which is so often waged in us, and in which resignation so often wins the day. It is a contradiction that calls our life in question. For without hope one cannot live; to live is to hope. *Dum spiro spero* (while and so long as I breathe, I hope). But life and hope are undermined and destroyed by resignation. Innumerable people rise in the morning, and no longer hope for anything from the new day. Young people switch to harder and harder drugs because they no longer have any hope, and therefore wish at least to have the immediate thrill and are ready to pay for it with their own worthless because futureless lives. To be old means for countless people the loss of all hope, and a mere vegetable existence prolonged to the last breath. People who are lifeless because hopeless surround us on all sides; they used to have hopes, but these have deceived them, and now they look back bitterly on their earlier illusions. Life begins with hope, and ends with hopelessness, it has not been worthwhile.

A hopeful look forward into the future, which does not deceive, does not explode as a soap bubble, does not *"make us ashamed"*, which does not at the end expose us to ridicule – that is what we need. The man who is called to such a hope, he can be a source of life, can work as a source of life on the crippled young and old people around him, as a source of life also for the good hopes by which people are moved to all kinds of good enterprises, to actions for the needy, to the struggle for a more human society, to the fight against armaments and war on the contemporary "day against war", to the fight against tyranny like that in Nicaragua – good enterprises that are yet so often beaten down and disappointed.

"Can hope be disappointed" was the theme of Ernst Bloch's first lecture in Tübingen when in 1961 he migrated from the east to the west. O yes, it can be bitterly disappointed. Some of us fought against Hitler and yet he came to power. We here in Dahlem hoped for a profound renewal of our nation through the defeat – and then the change was only rather superficial, and instead of its principles of peace the military blocs stand today in mutual confrontation, ready for a worse annihilation than Hitler was able to achieve. It was with great hopes that the students rose up ten years ago – and today at the University I am surrounded on many sides by a leaden fatigue, resignation, and spiritlessness, an educational and spiritual treadmill without any perspective of hope. For generations before us, men have hoped for the progress of mankind – and today instead of this, mankind seems to be sinking into barbarism. These were all good hopes, not false ones, and it was good to commit oneself to them. But all these hopes can be disappointed. We need the experience of a hope that does not desert us, so that we may be able to cope with the disappointment of good and great hopes, in order that, in spite of the disappointment, we may have the power to go on committing ourselves to the substance of the disappointed hopes.

That is the calling of Christians, to be a source of life against resignation. Our hope, hope in God, is not *opposed* to the hopes of which I have just spoken. The Gospel does not call us away from these hopes. It does not say to us, let go the hope of social justice and peace, of liberation from oppression, of overcoming the world of the war danger, the madness of armaments and world-hunger, and hope, only for yourselves, for eternal life! The Gospel says to us on the contrary, "You are called to a hope that will never put you to shame; you must share in these good enterprises and hopes, and collaborate in this world in the realization of good hopes, as a strengthening source of life for those who commit themselves to the cause, and especially because, protected from resignation by a hope which does not make you ashamed, you will not be dependent on experiences of success, and will be able to remain true and constant in the good cause, even when the hope of visible successes is disappointed".

"*We*", says Paul, we are in that situation. We have the equipment to be such a source of life. Our hope has a backbone that cannot be broken. Our hope does not let us down. With it, we shall never be put to shame. In all eternity there will be no moment when it can be refuted and cancelled out by a worse, disappointing reality. We shall never regret having relied on it, having depended on it. Whence has he this certainty?

He tells us in this passage, and you could understand these verses as revealing the source of this hope, which he promises to us with such certainty as our calling. But note; he does not give in them a proof for his hope, which one could verify externally, before deciding to participate in it. He only states, though clearly, what in fact was the source of the summons to hope that has reached him and the Church of Jesus Christ to which he is writing, the actual source of a life of hope which can penetrate as an element of life into a time of hopelessness. He says, we met Jesus – or, better, he met us – and that set in movement a quite improbable story of experiences, a story which Paul recapitulates in these verses: Jesus of Nazareth has through his Spirit made clear to us that he with his life, death, and resurrection is the final revelation, that is, the message of final truth and reality, the message concerning the final court of judgement that gives an ultimate verdict about the world and every one of us, to us and for us, the final, decisive word about our life, and indeed a wholly positive word. Jesus – it is well with us, God's thoughts for us are peace, full salvation. For us mistrustful creatures, who with good grounds do not trust anyone further than we can see him, and not even ourselves, and least of all the future, fate, nature and the stars. It is to us, the mistrustful that he gives the power to trust, to trust that God, the last court of appeal, who alone really has the last word, means well to us. Our knees give with fatigue, we lie down, and in despair give up, and cannot stand up again, but he raises us up, so that we can stand. Grace makes men that *stand*, that stand upright. He opens the door that gives access to the last mystery of the world, the mystery of life and of fate. God is mystery, yes indeed, but not a dark, closed, inaccessible mystery. God has a voice and ears, he makes himself heard, and he can hear us. God is *glory*, yes, but not a remote glory far away, high and indifferent to our misery, an inaccessible light above our darkness, but a glory that reaches down to meet us, a glory that is for us. We are on the way to sharing in his glory. If we make the venture of trusting in him, and living according to our calling in trust on him, then our life will be a journey towards his glory.

That is the meaning of the name Jesus Christ, a name of hope, a meaning of hope. And now with this hope, whither are we going? Not directly to heaven, but back into our earthly life, and that means into *tribulation*, into hopes that can be disappointed, into battles into which he sends us as his disciples, into the unpeaceful world as peacemakers, into solidarity with the hungry and the enslaved and the prisoners. In their presence he awaits us, and only in their presence can he be found by us, and we no longer complain how troublesome he makes our life, and we no longer complain about the defeats and disappointments. We are proud that we can be with him on his way, that he can use us for his cause that is beset with trouble on all sides in this world. His Spirit helps us not to grow slack in spite of all disappointments. It is a process of learning, we learn toughness and *endurance*. The opposition and the dangers can no longer impose on us. When we are struck to the ground, we rise again and again, and even at the grave we raise our hopes again.

We find by our experience that our endurance is greater than we had thought. What does not destroy us makes us stronger; contrary to expectation we stand the test because he protects us, and from all these experiences comes the hope which has led us along this way, a hope renewed, growing ever stronger, a hope no longer to be confounded, a hope which has passed through the stress of affliction, and can never be disappointed. It is not we who shall be put to shame, but all those who have tried to overthrow and refute it, and all those who believed that they could get through without it. The way of the love with which God has laid hold of our hearts, and led us into tribulation, is the way of a hope that cannot be disappointed, and will not be disappointed.

As such a group of hope, men of hope, we Jesus-people are of immeasurable importance for all the people without hope around us, for those who no longer hope for anything from life but the brief pleasure of drugs, or – and that is no better, for it also accords with the saying "let us eat and drink, for tomorrow we die!" – of making a career, and filling their bellies, and getting rich at the expense of others, ruthless, not seeing the poor Lazarus at their door. We are of importance also for those with whom we co-operate in activities which love enjoins upon us, for the victims of this time and this society, for the prisoners and the drug-addicts, for democratic rights, for peace. In all these activities hope can and will repeatedly be disappointed; therefore in them people are indispensible whose hopes are strengthened by the one hope that cannot be disappointed, and is not disappointed because it has its own basis and its backbone in the promise of the eternal God, in his promised support, in the living presence of God in Jesus Christ.

As I began to concern myself for today with these words of Paul, they sounded to me at first almost too great, and for that reason far away from our real life on this earth, that is so full of tribulations and disappointments. As I heard them as words telling of our calling, with which we are sent into this world for the sake of other people, and of the origin of this call, they spoke to me ever more clearly, particularly in relation to the despairs of this time. So I have now endeavoured to make this clear to myself and to you. A free translation will once more gather this together.

When we take risks trusting in him, we are on the right lines. God says "Yes" to our trust. When we do this we are truly at peace, in the midst of salvation. It is Jesus who brings us into trust, and thereby into *shalom*. Through him, now already, the door is open into grace, to God's life for us. Through him we can stand upright. We have a new self-confidence, and a new perspective of hope directed towards the splendid reality of God. In addition there comes to us a new relationship to the great pressure to which we are exposed. We no longer complain about it, we are proud of it. For this is clear to us that from this pressure, from these troubles comes endurance, from endurance comes character, and from our character comes fresh hope. But hope does not disappoint us, it holds us up, and will not let us go to pieces.

For now already God's Spirit is at work in us, and through him the love
of God which fills our hearts, our wills, and our thoughts, and sets them
in motion.

Vanguard of Peace

Eternal heavenly Father, you have named us as your sons and daughters through your Son, our brother Jesus. Now we no longer need to fear for our lives. Your life surrounds us even in the darkest hours, your life leads us through death to you, into life. But time and again we forget this. Therefore, time and again darkness becomes more powerful than your light. That is why so little life goes out from us to the others, who also do not know any more. Do not punish us, we pray you, for our forgetting, by withdrawing your word! Forgive us for our forgetfulness, lead us back into life through your word, that as your children we may serve you in all your human children in their manifold need here on this earth. Lord, have mercy on us!

When the past lies on us like a burden, when the present oppresses us, when the future makes us anxious, then we lift up our eyes to you. Lord, give us signs of your presence in the midst of the confusion of the world and our life! Indeed you give them to us. Make us observant of your signs, observant of the help you have given us, observant of the tasks with which you enrich our life every day! We pray that you will imprint your promises in our hearts to strengthen and direct us every day.

In Christ Jesus you are all sons of God, through faith. For as many of you as were baptized into Christ have put on Christ. There is neither Jew nor Greek, there is neither slave nor free, there is neither male nor female; for you are all one in Christ Jesus. And if you are Christ's, then you are Abraham's offspring, heirs according to promise.
Gal. 3, 26–29.

You are all God's children, all! Therefore everyone who for any reason has come here, even the man who when this assertion is made would now like to slip away, discouraged or defiant or indifferent. That helps no one; it is already established, it is a matter of fact. You are all the children of God! The expression is old-fashioned, but the thing is extremely up to date. The Hebrew language, to describe where one belongs, uses the figure of speech "son" or "child". If we call someone a "bird of misfortune", in Hebrew he is called a "son of misfortune", and if we say about someone that he is a lover of peace, and that peace emanates from him, the Hebrew language calls him a "son of peace", just as we call a man a "child of happiness" or a "Sunday child" or a "child of death". By this we mean where a person belongs, what determines someone's life, what is decisive for his life.

When I came in here, before the Apostle opened his mouth, I did not know this: *"You are all children of God"*, which means, you all belong to God's side, and that means, to the side of life, of righteousness, of fulfilment, of the future. When I came in, I did not know that. I am a man, a man who is growing old, death gets nearer to me every day, I am not a child of life. I observe from my cowardice, when there is a question of exposing myself on behalf of innocent people who are suffering injustice, I observe from my jealousy of people who have it better than me, who are more successful, and I observe from my zeal in forwarding my interests, that I am a child, not of righteousness, but of unrighteousness. And the person beside me, who makes life sour for me, who has deeply offended me, who is a burden on my life, he too is not a child of God, but like me, a child of death. Or we concede to ourselves mollifying circumstances, and say more modestly; we are just children of our conditions, products of this society, perhaps products of this society that sets men against men, this class society, competitive society, acquisitive society, or, still more modestly, we are just products of nature, products of this natural order, that brings us into existence and brings us to dissolution, and thus children of death, and everything else is illusion.

But that everything else is illusion, my friends, is a conclusion that has never satisfied many people, and understandably. There must surely, they thought, be a way from the side of death to the side of life. For this we have designed programmes, religious, moral, political, social and psychological ways to salvation and messages of salvation. The religions, all together, including the political and scientific religions of modern days, are in competition as to which is the better way across from the side of death to the side of life. And the people of that time who came into the Churches of Galatia which had been founded by Paul, wished to teach them a better lesson than the one that they had heard from Paul, and they said to the Churches, "The Gospel is in fact, as Paul has said to you, a splendid thing". Wherein does the splendour of the Gospel consist? It consists in this, that it is a splendid possibility of crossing from the side of death to the side of life, a wonderful offer of God. And now it depends on your going with us along this offered way, and that means, fulfilling the conditions that have been established for this transition from death to life, religious and moral conditions which are contained in the law of God, and then at last you will some day come to the point of having worked your passage from death to life, and will be able to say "Now we are children of life, no longer children of death, but children of life".

Note well; Paul does not approve of this at all. In this disturbed letter, Paul warns the Galatians not to understand the Gospel as a possibility, as a programme, even the best of programmes, which makes it possible for us to work our passage from the side of death to the side of life. Quite the contrary, Paul will not speak of a possibility; he tells us of a reality, not of a way from us to God, but of God's way to us, down to us in this God-forsaken world, not of how we may bring ourselves on to God's side. No, his Gospel is the great story about how God brought himself to our side, certainly by this means to bring us to his side, certainly by this means to open up new possibilities of life for us, but starting wholly from that point, from the reality of the presence of the life of God here on our side.

What then does life look like when our eyes are opened, as Paul would like to open them by his words, or at least contribute to their opening, so that we see our life with the eyes of the Gospel? I shall try to say that in the context of the whole New Testament. And in this situation I have in mind the different hard burdens of life of which some of you have told me in these last weeks. What does life look like then? I am surrounded by life, it bears me, it will not leave me or forsake me. Me, an ageing man, me whose dearest relative has just been attacked by cancer, me, a young man, driven hither and thither by his instincts and appetites, and by his perplexities, me a member of this human race, which today obstinately and blindly is working its own downfall, I am a child of life. And that alone is true, and everything that contradicts it is untrue; I am an heir of life!

Heir, that is the word with which Paul here closes. Who makes us his heirs? Whose heirs are we? The heir is death, death is the great inheritor of all things, says a Persian proverb. But here it says, *heirs of God*. Not in such a manner as one who becomes the heir of other people who die, as if we inherited from a dead God, but in the manner that children, from their earliest days, daily inherit and reap the benefits that their parents have earned by sacrificial toil. The Gospel is the story of the sacrifices and labours of God. Down to the darkest hour on Golgotha he has undertaken everything to make it possible for us to say "I am a child of life, I am an heir of life".

That holds good, and this is the place from which to start our thinking every day. And every day on which we rise and think it's no longer any use, and our life is wasted, and things won't change; every day is already changed on which you repeat that to yourself and take it seriously, and allow a power of change to enter into your life, and in the strength of this go into your environment as a messenger of life and a carrier of blessing. Then it will be our experience that we are richer than we know, we have more to hope for, and we are more helped than we believe, men of life and of blessings. To see life thus differently, to see it thus changed, to change it thus and lay hold of it thus, that is what faith means.

When Paul here says *"You are all children of God through faith in Jesus Christ"*, then you must not hear that with disappointment, as if in spite of all now a condition was being laid down, as one sometimes unfortunately hears the passage expounded. "Yes, this you must believe, and that you must believe, only *then* you will be saved, then God will be gracious to you, only then will you be a child of God." Not "must"! That would be a law, and a quite impossible law at that. For we can do anything sooner than compel and force ourselves to believe. Faith is the most impossible thing for us, if we believe that it is in our power. Faith is what arises in us, just as love and friendship and hope cannot be commanded and produced and manipulated by anyone in himself and by himself, but can only arise from what is given us in experience. So Paul does not believe that through faith we could or would make ourselves children of God. But he came, he has by his life

and all his sacrifices and labours put himself on our side, and thereby
made us his children, children of life, and now from day to day we are
allowed to have a little faith, that is, to open our eyes and see things as
his word shows them to us, and not tightly close our eyes or see life with
the eyes of unbelief. In that case the new reality, the sonship of God,
which is made real in Jesus Christ, cannot penetrate our life to change
it, then we remain messengers of death, instead of becoming messengers of life, and so the almighty God quite humbly, as it were on his
knees before us, pleads with us through the Gospel, that we might be
willing to be told that we are on his side, and that he is on our side, that
we are children of life, surrounded by life, that we might be willing to
take that as being more serious and real than anything which contradicts it.

Let his word more certain grow,
And though thy flesh protesteth "No!"
Still do not be afraid.

That is one thing, my friends. But there is something else in the text,
which is most closely connected with it. Paul is a very practical man.
The Gospel is a wholly practical matter, and the alteration in this world
which it sets out to make, is not merely an alteration in feelings and
thoughts, important though such an alteration is; it is an alteration in
circumstances. That is also in our text, and for this reason two things in
the text are to be noted.

Firstly, what I have been permitted to say to myself, and to you, that
holds good for me, but not only for me. For me too it holds good, and I
must hear it in order that my attitude to life today and tomorrow, and
my behaviour to other people should change. But in order that my
behaviour to other people may change I must also hear; it holds good
for me, but not only for me, but equally for all the others. You are all
God's children, *all!* That is the splendid *"all"* that runs through all the
letters of Paul. "For as in Adam all die, so also in Christ shall all be
made alive." (I Cor, 15, 22.) "So through the righteousness of one man
justification of life has come to all." (Rom 5, 19.) "And he died for all,
that those who live should live not for themselves, but for him." (2 Cor.
5, 15.) *All,* and by this we have first, as had the Galatians then, to think
of the people next us in the church here, that is, of the Christians next
us, all of them. Of the Christians who are important to us, to whom we
are grateful for the witness of their life, by whose strong faith we
so often encourage ourselves, and we must also think of the other
Christians with whom we have to find fault, who claim indeed to be
Christians, a claim with which however their life by no means agrees.
Every one is a child of God. To each one we must say "Since the
Gospel reached you, and you are baptized and drawn into the Church
of Christ, therefore God needs you in his band of messengers of life".
You are a child of God, and as such let him help you! There is no one
who stands within hearing of the Gospel of whom we must despair, nor
must we despair of any congregation not even of this congregation of

Dahlem, which once was a shining city set on a hill, and in which now so much languishes. In no place must we give up hope that life will spring up once more, where now there is feebleness.

But now we must not stop at the Christians. True, the Apostle Paul speaks of the Christians in Galatia. *"You are all children of God through faith in Jesus Christ."* But if we were to conclude from this, that only Christians were God's children, then we would add to the terrible system of privilege which has always been the blight of human history, something quite specially bad; the Christians as privileged possessors, being God's children and friends, and round about them a God-forsaken God-rejected abandoned world. That is quite contrary to the central drift of the whole Bible, which says: *He does not forsake his world.* Religious people may have unmerciful thoughts like this, but God's thoughts are not so unmerciful; he has given himself for all. He is not content with a few religious people in his heaven. He wishes to have back all those who have lost themselves in error, all the children of men, he wishes to have them as his children. And this gives us the right to see every human being as a child loved and sought by God, and then our behaviour to him will be profoundly changed. Then we cannot believe in his brutality, his indifference, in his eccentric convictions. All that is superficial, and we know that we have to stand up for him, and concern ourselves about him, and the world about us becomes full of tasks, because it consists wholly of God's children, to whom the life-giving message of God's fatherhood must be brought.

And the second thought: this is a practical message which changes behaviour and with it the conditions. One sees this from the fact that Paul very deliberately places certain groups of people together. He speaks of *Jews and Greeks.* These were then the privileged and unprivileged groups. The Jews had religious advantages over the Greeks. The *free* had a higher social standing compared with the *slaves*, who had absolutely no rights, and the *men* had always secured great advantages for themselves over the *women.* That is now at an end, says Paul. Our oneness in Christ as children of God signifies an end of the contrast between privileged and unprivileged, an end of the whole business of privilege. He means this not only in terms of cult and worship, when here in worship we come together at the Lord's Table, that there no social distinctions count, no national and racial distinctions, that negroes and white people, char-women and company directors and so on all meet together here, but that when people go out of Church everything is as it was. He also does not mean only that something changes in our feeling, that these separate groups of people united in Christ, now think in a friendly manner about each other, no longer maliciously, and do not hit each other on the head, but that still everything remains as it was. But he means really that now the business of privilege is at an end, since the privileged person surrenders his privileges, and the unprivileged person is lifted up to equality of rights. Only from this will peace be created. The fellowship of brotherly equality of rights is the vanguard of peace in a distracted world. Or to put it in modern, that is to say foreign, words, an egalitarian group as the model of an egalitarian society of the future.

Since it carries this message in itself, the Christian community is so disquieted by the divided state of the world, and by its responsibility for peace. Here in West Berlin there began last Sunday a Peace Week. Christian and non-Christian religious and political groups united to do something for peace, in order to bring a knowledge of peace into this former frontier town of Berlin, which now must become a town of peace, if it is going to have any significance in the future as a contributor to the knowledge of peace. In so doing it at once became clear to them as they set about their large-scale work of preparation; that peace does not only mean the absence of war between the States, but that the immigrant workers are a part of the problem of peace, and so is the problem of the homeless, and so on. Because the privileges to which some hold on grimly, which others are seeking, are the worst cause of dispeace among mankind. A young woman pastor told me last night that she has in her parish two communities, the large community of the upper and lower middle classes in their houses and rented flats, and beside them a settlement of homeless people. These are two quite different communities. Now she is struggling in the one community that it may recognize its unity with the settlement for the homeless. Now it is quite clear that it would be idle chatter if Paul were to say, "Here are not bourgeois and workers, here are not house occupiers and house owners and people sent to a settlement for the homeless, but all are one in Christ, if this happened only in worship at Church, and in feeling. For this young minister the question at once is: is our congregation a Christian congregation, is the difference between the bourgeois community and the settlement for the homeless really abolished? This makes it clear that this attack of Paul on the privileged, and this proclamation of a fellowship of the children of God, children of the same Father, and brothers of Jesus Christ, as a fellowship of true brotherly equality of rights, brings us before immense tasks and helps us perhaps also to cope with the individual tasks of our personal life, in which we are so often entangled. This too is a result of the promise "I am your life". You are children of life, and not of death. Therefore we pray you, who made us this promise and gave us the power to look at our life and apprehend it in this manner; help us now to put away despondency, and to find the courage to reckon with the presence of your life, and help us so that even the greatness of the tasks into which you send us with it may not discourage us! We are glad, Lord, that we have the privilege of being your children, children of life.

Lord, we hear your message, the message of life. Our heart begins to rejoice, begins to divine how much you wish to give us. Therefore we tell you now frankly all our doubts, confess to you what hinders us from believing your message and building our life upon it. You see better than we do everything that speaks against your word in this world of yours. We do not make a list of these things to you, but we mention before you especially the terrible suffering of the Biharis in Bangladesh, the great hunger in North Africa, the tortured in Turkey, in Brazil, in South Vietnam, the embattled and bristling enmity in the Near East, and the world's manifold suffering, and everything that holds people back, even in prosperity, from seeking after you and trusting in you. You know it, Lord. Now we ask you; impress on our hearts what we have heard with our ears, let it take effect in our life, make it too, take effect in the lives of others, and so lead the world-movements, that men everywhere may see in men their brother and your child. Create brotherly equality of rights among all men, and help us by our sacrifice and our work to make our contribution to it! Keep us from clinging to our privileges, our special rights and our wealth. Make our hearts free to sacrifice them and put them at the service of those who are under-privileged. We pray to you for the effectiveness of the Peace Week. Let it be a blessing to those who organize it, and to those who are reached by it, and may this work continue to spread in our city.

We pray to you for the dead whom we have accompanied to the grave, for Marie Anna Leo, and for all who in the coming week will undergo operations, for the sick in the hospitals, for the doctors, sisters and nurses.

We pray to you for the teachers, Professors, school children, and students, for the way to truth that they seek, and for fruitful knowledge for us all.

We pray to you for our Government; we pray to you for all who are lonely, oppressed, depressed, and have no other help but you. Send them help! And lead us all to that place in the world above where we may without ceasing apprehend the truth of your word, and without ceasing praise and bless you!

Cells of Renewal in the Threatened World

You follow after those who have run away from you, who have entangled themselves in error and guilt. You do not wait until we come to you. You seek us out where we are. You have entered into the misery of men, you have become one lost among the lost, in order to save the lost. Lord, we ask you, make your coming find its way into all our lostness and extremity. Make us to find again our place as brothers and servants of all men who have lost you. Lord, have mercy on us!

Lord, since we have heard how you seek the lost, we pray you: Awaken us that we may not let any man be lost! Make us through your Resurrection to look on dying and death with new eyes. Make us to find life in the certainty of your presence.

Do not be deceived; God is not mocked, for whatever a man sows, that he will also reap. For he who sows to his own flesh will from the flesh reap corruption; but he who sows to the Spirit will from the Spirit reap eternal life. And let us not grow weary in well-doing, for in due season we shall reap, if we do not lose heart. So, then, as we have opportunity, let us do good to all men, and especially to those who are of the household of faith. Gal. 6, 7–10.

The older people among us will remember how often the first verse of this passage *"Be not deceived, God is not mocked, for whatever a man sows, that he will also reap"*, was quoted in the years between 1933 and 1945. Hitler had success after success. With every success he and his followers became more arrogant and cruel. With every success the pressure increased on those whom he wished to set aside. With every success new sections of the public went over to his side, because many people thought that resistance was hopeless, and one must be there in good time in order to share in the harvest when success came. Only a small remnant remained that could not adjust itself to him, in whose ears there sounded these words with the question "What is being sown here, and what will the harvest look like?" And then one day things went so far, that those who previously seemed specially astute and had stood on the side of success, were exposed as the fools, and the others proved themselves to be the wise and far-sighted, who had known that bad seed would have a bad harvest.

So what the Apostle Paul says here is at first merely a simple, but very necessary, though often neglected, piece of popular wisdom. What is cleverness, real cleverness? Cleverness is breadth of vision and thought for the whole. Cleverness is reflection about the harvest which I am sowing with what I do now. For with what we do, we are sowing. Every one would agree with this metaphor of sowing. I purpose in what I do to produce a certain effect in the future. To be clever means to know that we always sow more then we intend, as now a young

physicist from Brunswick, Klaus Müller, explains in his most signifi-
cant book "The Prepared Time", to be clever means, not only to have
the intended results in mind and calculate them in our action, but also
the effects that our action has upon the whole context of life, on many
others, of whom we take no account, and with this, the repercussions of
our action upon us. We have sowed insecticide in order to get rid of
insects, and cause good harvests, but we have destroyed thereby the
life-context of the plants, which alone makes good harvests possible,
and no one had previously thought of that. We have canalized rivers in
order to make them passable by ships, in order to get rid of flooding.
The floods have gone, but the ground-water has also gone, and the
dryness is increasing. The white farmers in America caused negroes in
Africa to be hunted and transported over the sea, in order to have
cheap labour. The result corresponded to the intention, business
boomed, but the further result was the racist brutalization of American
society, the trigger of the Negro Question, all the insoluble problems
which bedevil that society today. We would have thought that clever in
Hitler's day, but we would never again consider the man clever who
only calculates on his effects, and is set on his immediate wishes, and
wishes to share in success today; we shall only call the man clever who
looks far ahead and thinks of the whole.

   Paul believes that cleverness has something to do with faith. And
that reminds us how, in the parables of Jesus to the disciples, the
people of faith, cleverness is repeatedly spoken of. Cleverness is a
virtue of faith; one can see this from the fact that cleverness in this
sense signifies a freedom. Someone might object, as I recently heard,
"What has cleverness to do with faith?" Christians are not cleverer
than other people, and intelligence is just as variously distributed
among believing people as among the godless. That is true, but we are
not speaking here about intelligence, cunning, craftiness. The people
who before 1945 were on the winning side were intelligent, highly
intelligent, and after 1945 they were exposed as fools. True cleverness
means breadth of vision, and breadth of vision is the freedom to lift
one's gaze beyond the pressures of today into an enduring perspective.
And true cleverness is thinking of the whole. That is the freedom of
breaking the fetters of my own interests, taking into equal consideration with my own the interests of others, realizing that I am only a part
of a whole, and thinking from that viewpoint. This cleverness is a mode
of freedom. In faith we are concerned with freedom. To believe means
truly to reckon with the reality of the living God. It is the reality of the
living God that creates the connection between seed and harvest.
Whether, in what we are doing today, and in the means that we use to
reach our profit, God comes in our way, whether in our action we have
God on our side or against us, that is what decides about the harvest.
Paul speaks of this here with a strange expression *"To sow unto the
Spirit"*. What is a man who sows unto the Spirit? That is a man who fits
in his action and his intention and his calculation and behaviour with
God's activity which is known to us through the Gospel, God's great

activity among his human race. A man who sows unto the Spirit, places himself and his action and his behaviour at the disposal of the Spirit, places himself at disposal as a messenger of the life-creating Spirit to other men. He will therefore no more tremble for his life. If I am a man who sows to the Spirit, then I am confident in spirit, i.e. I am no longer anxious about my life and I trust to the Spirit that he will give to my action the effect for which I ask him. If I am a man who lives in the Spirit, then it is repulsive to me to live at the cost of others, for I would wish to live together with others in peace and joy, I would rather that they lived at my cost. If I am a man who lives in the Spirit, then I turn away from means and methods that are contrary to the Spirit. If I am a man who lives in the Spirit, then I hold unswervingly fast to the promise of the Spirit, even if I have to bear harmful consequences for doing so. I hold fast to the promise *"they who sow unto the Spirit shall reap without losing heart"*.

A man who sows unto the flesh, what is he? The word *"flesh"* in the language of Paul, means not our body, nor yet our bodily needs, e.g. our stomach's needs, nor our sexual needs. "Flesh" in the language of Paul is man left to himself, who must fight his way through, because no one is on his side, and no one is concerned for him, who has no time to take thought for tomorrow, and has no power to think of others, because he is entirely possessed by the thought of asserting himself today. The man who sows unto the flesh puts his trust in any means and any method if only it promises success in keeping him on top. He is a man full of anxiety, because no one is on his side except himself. I think that every one of us will ever and again recognize himself in this man, who sows unto the flesh. Time and again I am this godless egotistical man, who holds himself to be clever and realistic, but is really narrow-minded, thinking nothing of the morrow, and disregarding and overrunning other people. It is already much, if through the influence that Jesus gains upon my life, time and again, making a new beginning every day, I desert from the side of the men of flesh, and put myself on the side of the men of the Spirit. And it is already much if in my life there are not only defeats of the Spirit at the hands of the flesh, but repeated victories of the Spirit over the flesh, victories of freedom from today's concerns and myself, freedom for tomorrow for the whole, for others.

To strengthen us in this, the Apostle Paul directs our vision forward to the harvest. *"He who sows to the Spirit will of the Spirit reap eternal life."* This prediction Paul sets against the prediction of the flesh. The prediction of the flesh runs thus: "He who sows to the Spirit will go under; only he who sows to the flesh will keep on top in the hard struggle for existence on this earth". That is sober realism, everything else is sentimentality, and the Bible itself also says so in Psalm 73 "I saw the prosperity of the wicked, for they do not live in trouble; their bodies are sound and well-nourished. What they say must be as though spoken from heaven, and what they say counts on earth. Therefore the people run to them, and men stream to them in crowds, like water. The godless are always lucky, they become rich." And the man of flesh in us says "Yes, that's how it is. He who sows to the Spirit goes under, only the man who sows to the flesh keeps on top."

The word of Paul about sowing and reaping reminds us of two things today. First, of the lesson, which, as I said at the beginning, we Germans have experienced in the most recent past. In the days of the capitulation in 1945, we went past the quarters of the S.S. and the Gestapo. They had commandeered the finest villas in the towns through which we came. Here, as unbridled masters, they had tyrannized over a frightened populace. And now they stood before these villas, some of them drunk, others sober, and looked at us passing infantrymen with eyes in which dwelt emptiness, in which there was nothingness, and which I shall never forget all my life long. Behind them their seed, and before them the harvest of what they had sown, restitution, imprisonment, and death. They envied us Tommies who marched past, who were going into captivity, and none of us would have liked to be in their shoes.

That is the one connection between seed and harvest, to which this word of Paul's relates, when he predicts, "Through this, through sowing to the flesh, you will come to ruin". And this word today receives still more confirmation – I must always come back to the same point – in the immense dangers to humanity which we comprehend under the title of "the ecological catastrophe". What we mean by this is not a sequence of natural events, but the consequence of a million human acts of sowing, which has been building up and building up for centuries, and increasingly in our century; irresponsibility, manifold forms of greed and dancing round the golden calf, lust for power and enjoyment of power, exploitation of human beings and exploitation of nature, cowardice in the face of the powerful, all put together, this thinking only of today and one's own little life, multiplied a million-fold. This "sowing to the flesh" will be your destruction, says Paul. Today this is continuing, this blind activity, in spite of all alarming reports in the newspapers. And we have not got nearly so far as to be able at least to say, "The Christians are alert, the Christians have become clever, the faith of Christians is in order, and therefore so is their cleverness, and therefore they have broken out of this bondage to today and their own selves".

Now let me say this in addition. In order to help us to break out of these fetters, Paul brings in an element with which rigidly consistent thinkers have always found fault. He says "*He who sows to the Spirit will reap eternal life*". Rigidly consistent thinkers like the great philosopher Immanuel Kant found in him and similarly in the reward-ethic of Jesus, as it has been called, a relapse into eudaemonism, and that means in English a relapse into an attitude where once again everyone is only seeking for his own advantage, and does not do the good for the sake of the good, but because of the advantage that he has in doing so, either for the sake of earthly prosperity, or for the sake of heavenly salvation. In fact Jesus and Paul do not say with lofty austerity, you must do the good for the sake of the good, and must take no thought about what will result for you from doing so. But very mercifully they accept the anxious and dangerous question that inevitably rises in us, the question "If I must not think of today, and my own interests, what will happen to me and my little life, on which, for all that, I depend?" And because this question can again drag us back into every kind of narrow-mindedness and blindness and wickedness, therefore Jesus and Paul accept it, and with all emphasis and understanding lay their hands on our shoulder and say "provision is made for you, have no fear, eternal life surrounds you, eternal life stands ready for you. You will not regret having sowed, not to the flesh, but to the Spirit. And even if, in the dangers which threaten anyone who resolves to follow Jesus and to sow to the Spirit, you have to forfeit your life, you will not regret it, eternal life surrounds you, eternal life will be your harvest. The other harvest is nothing but destruction and death." Thus encouraged we take heart again.

Thus the other danger in addition to fear for my life is at least in some small degree repelled, and must certainly be constantly repelled, namely the danger of exhaustion, of resignation. Paul indicates it when he says *"Let us not grow weary in well-doing"*. There will be so many reverses. We have so many unfortunate experiences with men to whom we do good. The power and the resistance of universal wickedness, blindness, and narrow-mindedness in the individual life and in politics is so great, that the situation looks quite hopeless. *"To sow unto the Spirit"* means, to listen anew to the promise. To sow unto the Spirit means to trust in the promise. Without this promise we would fall victims to resignation. But now we have something in which we can trust, now we have something for our faith, the promise which accompanies us and keeps us wakeful, and when someone gives up, he must at once say to himself "now there is something wrong with my faith". And when something is wrong with my faith, then there is only one remedy, namely to return to the place where faith can be born, to the promise.

From all this we note, that in the situation today what is necessary for mankind, is a profound metanoia, and that means that not penitence, but only a profound change of heart, a thoroughgoing change in our behaviour in every sphere of life can save a threatened humanity. That gives to the Gospel today a tremendous practical significance, such as it has never had before. Where you begin to sow to the Spirit, and where even a very small congregation and Christian group begins to sow to the Spirit, it becomes a cell of renewal in threatened humanity, there new life begins even in this small fragment, and will then also work outwards and rouse others to new behaviour, to new movements, such as are necessary today.

One more thing in closing; the last words can disappoint us, for there it says, *"So then, as we have opportunity, let us do good to all men, especially to those who are of the household of faith"*. Here one or other of you whose eyes today are directed, as they should be, to the whole of mankind, might be disappointed with Paul, who, as soon as he had widened our vision to include all men, now again confines it to the Christians, to Church members, to like-minded people, "fellows in the faith".

Does that mean that we should give only for Church purposes, or only for the support of hungry Christians, and not for the other hungry people? And that we should pray only for Christians in distress, when someone is persecuted for the sake of faith? Or does Paul think that at any rate we should first relieve distress within the Church, and then, with the rest of our time and our powers, as far as it is possible, help the others too? Certainly not, I think. That would be wholly contradictory to the great urge towards totality which is characteristic of the whole Bible. But, I think, Paul means this; If things are not right among you in the congregation, then they will not be right in your relation to the outer world. When among you in the congregation – and think of the congregations of that time with slaves and a deprived proletariat and more prosperous people all mingled together – it can happen that people are starving, and people are treated with violence, and you do not trouble yourselves about it, then certainly nothing will be done about what I spoke of first – about *"doing good to all men"*. If we, to take an example, continue to baptize children in settlements for the homeless – and we hold fast by infant baptism in our national Church, whether rightly or wrongly – then they are our "comrades in the faith", and then they blame us because they grow up and are inwardly destroyed by their conditions of life. But when we begin – I mention here only this example – to concern ourselves for the children in the settlements for the homeless here in Berlin, then things will inevitably go further, then the whole disgrace of the slums in our wealthy city will become intolerable to us, and so everywhere. And if we arbitrarily confine ourselves to pastoral care, or care of Christian families, then we would not really help these brothers. We can only help individual brothers and sisters if we attack general situations of need, and that leads irresistibly further, a Church must be truly solidary with the whole world in its need of help.

Therefore we pray to our Lord, that with his Holy Spirit he would lead us from day to day to acts of liberation, helping us to look beyond our today and our insignificant selves, to be filled inwardly with the power of the Holy Spirit that not only teaches us to recognize prudence, but to do prudently, so that we may be salt and light among this threatened humanity of ours. Help us to do this, our Lord!

Salvation for All

God desires all men to be helped, and to come to the knowledge of the truth. I Timothy, 2, 4.

"That all men should be helped." Who knows a better wish, a more beautiful dream, a brighter vision? We think of ourselves, we think of those among our acquaintance who at the moment are in a particularly difficult situation. We think of the twelve to thirteen million refugees in the world, whose numbers are now increased by the refugees from Afghanistan. We think of the anxiety with which this time we changed the calendar because the shadows of the threat of war have again become so much darker. In contrast with that, the prospect *"that all men should be helped"*. A splendid utopia, isn't it? Utopia means a vision that has no place on earth. And that is precisely the case, that all men should be helped has no place on earth. On the contrary, that contradicts the law that holds good on earth, the more each helps himself, the less all are helped, the more people come to grief. Where one man helps himself, he thrusts others down, where one strives upwards, to a place in the sun, he thrusts others into darkness. The programme is utopian, all cannot be helped.

On the other hand, do we really wish that *all* should be helped? Or do we wish it only in the first moment, and so soon as we reflect on it more carefully exclude some from it? Are our enemies also to be helped? Even the people of whom we think with deep anger? Are even the Bolshevists to be helped? The unbelievers? To the question "who shall be helped?", men have ever answered by drawing boundaries – not these, and not those. Christianity in particular has distinguished itself by means of such boundaries, and employed Jesus' words about the eye of a needle and the narrow gate in order to formulate all kinds of conditions which must first be fulfilled before one belongs to those who are to be helped, whether the conditions are those of good works, or even the condition of right belief. People have pictured God in the likeness of the Ministry for Social Security, which always first tests whether a person is worthy of support.

In the place of such drawing of boundaries to which God must submit, and which were proclaimed in God's name, the door is here thrown wide open: *everyone is to be helped.* Peace on earth not only hominibus bonae voluntatis – not only to men of good will, that was a mistranslation by the Latin Version of the Bible – the Vulgate – but as joy that will come to *all* people, and so even to those who are still of evil will. They too are to be helped. Note well how when this purpose and programme is formulated, our idea of the men of evil will changes; they are regarded as sick men who must be helped to get rid of their illness. Not as men who make themselves evil, and must be punished for that, but as men who are in deep distress. Their wickedness is regarded as their distress, and therefore it is proclaimed that they too, yes, they especially, are to be helped.

And yet that is the real meaning of the word "forgiveness of sin": a sinner is not someone who through misadventure has made a mistake, or one who beside all sorts of good qualities has unfortunately shown some faults; a sinner is, if the word is to be taken as seriously as in the Bible, and then in the Reformers' interpretation of the Bible, a homo malae voluntatis, a man of evil will. To him the Christian message of peace does not apply, if it only forgives the man of good will. But if we are all called sinners, then we are all declared to be men of evil will, and then indeed it has been a great, almost inconceivable mistake that precisely in the history of Christianity, the zeal for drawing boundaries, of making reservations, of requiring the condition of good will, of making exclusions, has got such a hold, with all the devastating consequences of burning of heretics, and extirpation of Indians and persecution of Jews, where under the light of the Gospel it ought to have been evident that if God begins to make exclusions from the number of people who are to be helped, then I too shall be excluded, *I* shall only be helped if *all* are helped.

The promise is glorious, the programme is glorious, and God is glorious, whose programme this is here declared to be. We should first of all reflect on this, before we give room to the questions which at once come into our minds when we think of this programme. Just as we come to know a man from his life programme, so it is with God. At any rate concerning the God about whom the Bible speaks, in the face of such all-embracing fundamental declarations as are given to us in this verse, we can never again say that we know nothing for certain about him and his will. That may be the case with the God of whom the philosophers speak, that may be true of fate, which many people confuse with God. But of the God, at any rate, with whom we have to deal through Jesus, we know exactly what he wants. He is one who wishes all men, and especially the sinners, the men of evil will, to be helped. In the preceding verse of this section of the letter, he is called *"God, our Redeemer"*, or, as one can also translate, *"God, our Saviour, wishes that all men be saved"*. Saviour and helper, that is our definition of God, and if Voltaire said mockingly of the God of Christian faith, "Forgiveness is his métier", then we can answer, "Yes, indeed, thank God, so it is"; saving, forgiving men of evil will, that is his métier, that is what he has made his business, that is the biblical definition of God.

Because this will is called *the will of God*, then the message of our motto for the year, spoken every day of this year, which has begun so alarmingly, means: It is not only your will that is present, your sometimes evil, sometimes good, but mostly rather mixed will, that is present and takes effect, and not only the will of the mighty, the people in Washington and Moscow, their bad, good, and for the most part rather mixed will, that makes world history. Another will has to be taken into account, another will mixes with it and takes effect, and that is not merely a brief and temporal will of transitory men, that is the will which is the source of us all, through which we came into existence, and that is the will that is going to prevail in the end, when the brief transitory will of mortal men will have nothing more to say. And this will, which is the origin of the whole universe, this will does not regard us as insignificant flies of a day, with lofty indifference, this will does not select for itself only a few fortunate examples of this questionable species of living things called men, and let the rest return to the ash-heap of death. This will desires that all men be saved – a will of love to us insignificant crippled flies of a day, with much evil in us.

And, be it noted, we are not dealing merely with a beautiful well-meaning wish, but with a serious will and resolve. Even in our case there is a great difference between merely wishing something, and seriously willing it. In wishing I dream, without commitment, how fine it would be, if . . . To give only one of innumerable examples; how fine it would be, if we had a school which did not destroy the nerves and character of our children! If I do not merely wish that, but *will* it, then I go into action. I am ready to pay something for it, then I commit myself, and risk something for it, my behaviour in life is determined by it, in a word, it has real consequences for my life. The message of this year's motto – a summary of the whole Gospel, all the stories and teaching of the Bible, the core of every service of worship, the intention of every word of the liturgy, of the hymns, together with Baptism, the Lord's Supper, and the Burial Service, is from all eternity the will to which the whole universe owes its existence, the will of the Creator, directed straight at you and me and everyone around us, with full resolve to save you and me and everyone around us, to give us fundamental help to a new life, such as that Will had in mind when it gave us life.

That message is announced to us as the truth about us every day of the new year. How is such help to be given to us? *"that we should come to a knowledge of the truth"* it says here. "What is truth?" we ask pensively and sceptically with Pilate. The motto for the year gives a quite clear and definite answer, precisely what has already been said *"God our Saviour wishes that all men should be helped"*. Not all sorts of truths out of the natural and supernatural world, not the truths about which the Pope and Hans Küng are in conflict, as to whether the Pope is wholly, or partly, or not at all infallible, whether Jesus "possesses the rank and dignity of God" and the like, also not a philosophical abstract truth in itself, but the truth of the divine programme, all are to be helped, I and you, and every one of our neighbours.

The knowledge of this truth is itself the saving help which is intended for us. But the knowledge of this truth is obviously not so easy to get as other knowledge of other truths, for example the truths we concern ourselves about in the University in research and teaching. We notice this by our resistance to this message. All of you, especially if you have listened well, can hardly go on listening when I go on so long describing this message, and do not let myself be interrupted by your questions, which have for a long time been eager to find expression in interruptions. If that is a serious, resolute will – how does that relate to the reality in which we are living, and in which we see countless people around us, who are obviously not being helped, who are either the victims of the evil will of man, or themselves giving expression to an evil will, and often enough both things in one person, victim and agent. Where then is this help and salvation? If there is a serious will of God, is it perhaps only a feeble will?

Where are you, universal consolation
In whom all mortals trust for their salvation? –

as we recently sang in the season of Advent, and then once more at Rudi Dutschke's funeral. Perhaps it was quite wholesome for us, limited by the time of one sermon and one service, to be compelled merely to hear this message of the motto for the year, to make it clear to ourselves, and not to give voice to our queries and objections, our whole difficulty in face of this great and beautiful message.

When I have to preach here again on the 3rd of February, we shall think once again about it, and then confront it with our reality, which looks so different, and from which our objections and questions arise. Meanwhile, however, let us go home and keep it as did Mary, of whom we are told in the Christmas story that she "kept all these things, pondering them in her heart". (Luke 2, 19.) Let us ponder in our hearts what is laid down for us so unquestionably as an unshakable truth: God – that is the one who wills that all men should be helped. If we believe that of him, and trust him – what would that change in the bearing and behaviour of our life in the unforeseeable events of this year?

1. I have beside me a helper. Whatever may happen, I shall not be lost. From this new trust grows daily new hope as daily bread for every day.

2. My neighbours and all men are to be helped in this way in the afflictions of their lives, even in the affliction of their evil will. If God helps me to faith, if he helps me, to become a man or a woman who is a servant of Jesus, then he helps me to be an instrument of his help to other people. I am to be helped in order that I may help others.

3. Trusting in his help, we learn the important difference between the right way to help ourselves, how we should do it as people who are responsible for our life, and the wrong way to help ourselves. The wrong way is the way of unbelief, the desperate manner in which we exploit other people, when we do not believe that God will help us, in order to save our lives at the expense of other people. From faith comes the right way to help ourselves, so that my neighbour can live with me, and I can help him to achieve his life with my life, which I am myself achieving in trust on God's help.

An Answer is Promised to our Prayer

Every word gets its more precise meaning only through the sentence in which it stands, and every sentence only from the group of sentences in which it stands. So also we can only truly grasp the significance of the sentence which forms the motto of the year 1980, when we know the context, and in any case questions should only be asked when one has to some extent understood an assertion. We heard the assertion of the year's motto three weeks ago *"All men are to be helped"* and *"God is he who wishes that all men should be helped"*. The context in which this stands is as follows:

First of all, then, I urge that supplications, prayers, intercessions, and thanksgivings be made for all men, for kings and all who are in high positions, that we may lead a quiet and peaceable life, godly and respectful in every way. This is good, and it is acceptable in the sight of God our Saviour, who desires all men to be saved and to come to the knowledge of the truth. I Tim. 2, 1–4.

So prayer, speaking with God, has a political importance. We ought to put some confidence in prayer. Prayer gets a double promise. Prayer can change us ourselves, our attitude to people and events: it can bring us out of a negative attitude to a positive one, from hate, rage, and fear to quiet and hopeful reflections and actions. And prayer can contribute to change even in political developments, in the direction of peace – *"a quiet and peaceable life"*, that is, to a life without threat and fear for our existence, such as we all long for. That is a promise! Note well, a promise that does not admit of calculation, for which one cannot demand proofs before one relies upon it, whose challenge one must rather at once follow, putting aside all doubts and questionings. Thus we must begin with prayer, talking over everything with God, with supplication and thanksgiving. To pray – and then of course to go on to action; ora *et* labora, pray *and* work! Pray and then do something for the cause for which you have prayed! Prayer gives power to action, particularly when action seems difficult or without prospects of success. Our prayer is promised an answer.

If we take this promise seriously and act upon it, it can change us today in a way that is urgently necessary for us. Today, when we have begun this year for which this year's motto has been selected, in a profound world convulsion, in which the word "war" which has become an unthinkable, inconceivable word, is in the newspapers every day. Today, when we are told how the third world war will one day start – or how it – none of us knows that – is already beginning. "In the nation the fear of war is growing" is the headline of the leading article of the present number of "Zeit" (31.1.1980). "Possibility that we are sliding into war" was lately one headline of a "Spiegel" interview with Willy Brandt, and in the same number of the "Spiegel" stood the frightening statement "It is a threateningly unstable, highly explosive political landscape of the 'eighties' which has been taking shape in the last fortnight . . . That their actions . . . , could create within days such a world-scene, neither of the two powers involved have known with any certainty – that only makes matters worse . . . The two great powers proved themselves incapable of estimating their own position and that of their opponents, and taking appropriate action – a lack of capacity on a scale which no one had expected" (Spiegel 14.1.80). So the third world war starts, for which no one wished, but everyone is to blame. If there are any survivors after it, – how many may there be, to whom one might then read their words and resolutions before the outbreak of war, without their sinking into the earth in shame and disgrace and remorse, all the *"rulers and those in high positions"* the intriguing politicians, the writers of newspapers, the after-dinner speakers – all those who today drive up rearmament which will destroy us either before the third world war or in it?

To an especial degree however the avoidance of war depends on a small number of *"rulers and those in high positions"*, on their wrong or right calculations, their calm or panic. The worst, most dangerous statement among all that I have read in these weeks, was for me President Carter's announcement that he would by all means ensure that the U.S.A. remains "the strongest nation on earth". Whoever says something of this kind, in the west or in the east, wishes to retain or reach superiority when according to the statements of our politicians peace at the present moment depends on the balance between the two super-powers. The man who sees his pride and his security in being the strongest, the man who is afraid to be in the same situation as all the rest of us, who belong to the weaker states, wishes for a superiority that must cause fear in the others, and thereby intensifies the mutually contending process of rearming, and is blind to the chief political task of today, which another President of the U.S.A., J. F. Kennedy has formulated "Either we gid rid of war, or war will get rid of us".

What can we do in this situation? The text which contains our motto for the year answers, "Yes, ask with all seriousness what each of you can do here, and do what you find with all your heart". But in all your doing, do not forget one definite kind of action of which even the feeblest is still capable: those who are in authority have urgent need of it, that the people under them pray for them. The rulers are not masters of the situation, and they are not their own masters; that we have just seen. They are incurring now already a vast burden of guilt, and will incur more if they go on like this. Their task is not to strive to be the strongest nation, they have the task of ensuring that people may be able to lead a *"godly and respectable"* life. People have said in criticism that the pupil of Paul who is supposed to have written this letter, is setting up a homely petty-bourgeois idea for life. But it seems to me that he is simply naming the minimum which the rulers and those in authority should seek to provide, that the people under them should not be forced to share in all the criminal acts which the Germans allowed to be forced upon them in the Nazi years, criminal acts which are today being devised in the armament laboratories, practised in the armies and perpetrated in war, but that the people under their authority should be able to live a godly and peaceable life, should have freedom to believe and to love without injuring others, and live in honour without having to destroy their fellow-men.

The most endangered of men today are the *"rulers and those who are in high position"*. They need our criticism, our opposition, *and* our prayers. Their spirit must be purified, illumined, drawn away from what is evil, encouraged in what is good. For this we ought to pray much more, all our political thinking ought to be permeated by this prayer, it is part of our guilt that we fail in this duty. Therefore this challenge to prayer is a question concerning our Christianity, our faith. What do we really think about prayer, what do we really think about the God to whom Jesus prays, and to whom to pray without ceasing he teaches and challenges us?

He is a "Saviour God", a redeeming God, the God who wills that *"help should be given to all men"*, the year's motto says to us. That means in any case, and without possibility of denial, that he is a God who hears. Our prayers do not echo vainly in the void. Our intercession is heard. He too thinks of those for whom we pray with all loving care, and the fact that he thinks of them makes our intercession not superfluous. For we are privileged to speak with him, as Luther says in his Small Catechism, "as dear children with their dear Father", and surely it would be unnatural if children, where the relation is right, did not speak with their father and mother about everything that is on their hearts, and if they did not ask the parents for their help. And indeed they have the right to put their own questions to him, who promises to help them.

If it really is God's will that all men should be helped, why then do we often see so little of this help, why do we see so many people entangled and destroyed in their affliction, even in the affliction of their evil will? Is he powerless in his will to help, as we often are; is his will genuine but not almighty? This was our question three weeks ago. One of those present at the service pointed out to me that in this case we are thinking of a help which is not at all intended here, namely a material bodily earthly help. But here what is said, translated exactly, was "that all men should be *saved*", and that this refers to our eternal salvation, the salvation of our souls, and our fellowship with God. Anyone who is not satisfied with that, or who has no interest in the salvation of his soul, should take that seriously. "For what is a man profited if he shall gain the whole world and lose his own soul" says Jesus (Matt. 16, 26). To lose his own soul – that means to be eternally separated from God, and "soul salvation" – this now old-fashioned word can be translated for modern men who are not accustomed to let their thoughts range beyond death, as an indestructible meaning for my life through fellowship with God, so that no death, no sufferings, and no war can separate me from the love of God. Yes, such salvation of the soul, such indestructible meaning, such eternal life in God is God's grant to all men, and for this all of them are to be saved. But here too the question returns "Are they then all saved, at least in this sense, for this soul-salvation?" Does God use his omnipotence so that they may all be saved for eternal life? This is termed the great question of Universalism, and we have not the time now to treat it as it deserves. But we see that in both cases the question arises of God's omnipotence, whether we are now thinking of earthly wellbeing or eternal salvation.

The theologians are of course always concerned with the question why God does not use his omnipotence so that what he wills may happen, that really all men may be helped, or that at least all men may be saved for eternal life. Many of them have here given the answer that God restrains his omnipotence because he respects our free will. For this reason he makes the realization of that which he wills dependent on our willing it also. I do not know if this explanation gives you some help. In my opinion it is a little too reasonable. I am more inclined to give Luther's answer. He thought that the contradiction which sticks in our teeth here, is quite insoluble for us here on earth. For it is the contradiction between God's will for salvation which he has made known to us in Christ, and the reality of the world which we see around us, and which must also be supported by the will of God.

For this reason Luther spoke of a "hidden will" of God, i.e., of a will of God which we cannot decipher and understand, and Luther thought that because this will of God is quite hidden from us, therefore God tells us in the Gospel that we ought not to brood over it, but should hold first to his revealed will, which we can know through Jesus Christ and in Jesus Christ, his will to salvation whose purpose is that all men should be saved. Therefore, faced by this alternative *either* we despair about this contradiction between God's loving will and the reality of the world, and are destroyed by it because we hold on to the reality of appearances, *or* we welcome God in Jesus Christ. In Jesus Christ, God, suffering himself, enters into this contradiction, Jesus Christ is the one who dies because of this contradiction, and in this contradiction holds fast to God's promises, and as the risen one proclaims to us the victory of God's love over all that contradicts it.

Jesus, dying because of the contradiction, did not cry on the Cross, as his words are frequently translated, "My God, my God, why hast thou forsaken me?" Translated exactly from the Hebrew, what he cried was "My God, my God, for what purpose hast thou forsaken me?" "What was in your mind in doing this? What can be the meaning, the outcome of this dreadful fate that you have allowed to come upon me?" Jesus' resurrection says to all of us; in everything that happens, God does nothing unmeaningful, even when it appears to us to have no meaning. When some day we pass from faith to sight, then we shall have left the contradiction behind us, then all tears will be wiped away, and all questions be silenced. God's omnipotence and God's promise will have become one in the final victory of the love of God.

But what now? No, rather, what follows from this now? What is the purpose of God's forsaking us, as it seems to us? That we may all the more flee to God. To what end does God appear to be silent? In order that we may all the more intently listen to that source where he lets himself be heard. What is the reason why reality seems to contradict his promises? That we may hold all the more fast to his promises. What is the purpose of his making us say that it really is his will that help should come to all men? That we may be co-workers and instruments of his help, and no longer instruments of destruction. Why does he invite us to make intercession? So that even when we seem to be quite helpless, we have something that we can do, something that makes sense. Why does he lay such special stress on our intercession? That in our faith and prayers we may not become egoistically self-centred, forgetting others, but may plead as priests for all men, especially for those in peril above us. Why does he promise us to answer our prayers? In order that we may know that we are not alone even when we are quite alone – that above all when we help, when we fight for peace and against the wickedness and folly of men, we are not alone, even when all our best efforts seem to achieve nothing.

Theoretically this is not a satisfactory answer, practically it is the best answer; it contains everything that is now unconditionally necessary for us; it is preparation for whatever may happen in this time of the danger of war, of armament for war and the irresponsible incitement to war and to armament. *"God wills that all men should be helped"*, with this we are told what in the year 1980 we have to do and what not to do, where we should collaborate, and where we should not collaborate, where we must place our reliance in life and in death.

Fellow-Workers With Love

For this is the message which you have heard from the beginning, that we should love one another, and not be like Cain who was of the evil one and murdered his brother. And why did he murder him? Because his own deeds were evil and his brother's righteous. Do not wonder, brethren, that the world hates you. We know that we have passed out of death into life, because we love the brethren. He who does not love remains in death. Any one who hates his brother is a murderer, and you know that no murderer has eternal life abiding in him. By this we know love, that he laid down his life for us; and we ought to lay down our lives for the brethren. But if any one has the world's goods and sees his brother in need, yet closes his heart against him, how does God's love abide in him? Little children, let us not love in word or speech, but in deed and in truth.

By this we shall know that we are of the truth, and reassure our hearts before him whenever our hearts condemn us; for God is greater than our hearts, and he knows everything. Beloved, if our hearts do not condemn us, we have confidence before God; and we receive from him whatever we ask, because we keep his commandments and do what pleases him. And this is his commandment, that we should believe in the name of his Son Jesus Christ and love one another, just as he has commanded us. All who keep his commandments abide in him, and he in them. And by this we know that he abides in us, by the Spirit which he has given us.
I John, 3, 11–24.

We find a point of departure in this long section of the letter when we take up a question contained in it (v. 17) and apply it to ourselves: *How does God's love abide in us?* What kind of people are these, who ask this question? When are we people who ask this? Surely, when "the love of God" is not a mere empty word to us, not merely a singular assertion made about singular pious people, something distant and quite unimaginable, but when it has already come near to us, has become something alluring, for which we long and which we desire. There can also be times when it becomes an empty meaningless word to us. These are the saddest times of our lives. But there can also, thank God, be times when this word touches our heart, and awakens the longing: "How if this were real, God's love to us, to me? How happy I would be!" And there can be times when a thrill of joy in us answers to this word, "Yes, it is splendid, thank God, God's love surrounds us and is the source of my life, we are loved". The love of God – what can that mean? Over and above the love of human beings which we sometimes are happy to experience, for which we long, without which we cannot live, and which time and again we have to do without – at the end, when the beloved person is taken from us by death – over and above this love from human beings and to human beings, there surrounds us and carries us a greater love which does not die, which even in death does not let us go, and from which nothing can separate us, "neither death nor life, neither angels nor principalities nor powers, neither things present nor things to come, nor height nor depth nor any other creature" (Rom. 8, 38). Still further; the whole universe with its countless starry worlds, even all its terrors, is surrounded and carried by infinite love, whose desire is to help all its creatures to the best.

Is that a beautiful dream, daily refuted by all the terrible things in the world? It might be so. That is a temptation, which continually assails us. What decides people like this letter writer who speaks with such radiant certainty about the love of God, against such a conclusion? Whence do such people draw their joy about the love of God? He only gives us an indication of it, but he knows that all his readers will at once understand and thankfully assent *"By this we know love, that he laid down his life for us."* (v. 16.) A man has sacrificed himself for us, and that was not merely a human sacrifice; in him the Eternal Love itself became man, in him the Eternal Love has sacrificed itself for us, and by this we know *that* Eternal Love directs itself towards us, and by what here happened we know also *what* love is, not a mere feeling, always an action, an action for others, down to the last consequence, down to the last sacrifice. That is love *"in deed and in truth"* (v. 18). And that is the final truth and reality about our life, and about the whole world, that is the state of affairs which we must and shall make our starting-point now; that is the message, the glad message which now goes through this dark world and invites all men to believe it, that is, to rely on it with complete assurance; we are beloved, eternal love surrounds and carries us. The man whose heart this message has touched, the man who longs for this, and rejoices in it, he is the one who wishes above all things that this love may never leave him, that it may remain in him, that is, that it may fill his heart with certainty and joy, and that he may remain in it, may draw his life wholly from it, in harmony with it, and radiating it to other people. But then it can happen, that this can become an urgent question to a man, how does the love of God remain in us?

How can this question arise? When does this become for us a question, an urgent question? A contradiction drives us to ask that question, a contradiction that has already brought "that one" to death, that man Jesus. He did not merely die, he let himself be put to death. So there are people who put to death, there is Cain, there are men who *"murder"* their brothers, as it says here (v. 12), with a strong word that is shockingly confirmed daily by the newspapers. Daily people are murdered, the world is full of murder and hate, and where men live in murder and hate, there they do not only spread death around them, they are themselves dead in the midst of life. *"No murderer has eternal life abiding in him"* (v. 15). *"He who does not love, remains in death"* (v. 14) he has death in himself instead of eternal life.

People who are apprehended by the reality of the love of God, are by no means carried up into heaven into a carefree, idyllic life. On the contrary, they continue to live in the world, and see this world in a far worse light, with far fewer illusions than before, as a world ruled by death, as a world filled entirely by dead men, and men who spread death, who only appear to live. *"We have passed out of death into life, because we love the brethren"* (v. 14) – and discover ourselves as living men in a world of dead men. A Russian Bishop who was shot in the civil war by soldiers of the Red Army, called out to these soldiers "Farewell, dead men! I am going into life". In the moment of his death he was a living man among the dead.

That is indeed a great self-confidence, and it could also lead to a great arrogance, and has repeatedly done so, to an arrogant contempt for these men of death around us; we are the chosen and the saved ones, we stand far above those wolves and sons of Cain, we sun ourselves in the love of God and are far better than these murderers. But the distressing question for us arises, when after the first discovery that this world is a Cain-world full of dead men, a second discovery follows: even we, though we have come to faith in the love of God, and thereby have crossed over from death to life, even we are still a piece of this Cain-world. Even we, as lambs of Christ, as messengers of the new life, sent among the wolves, howl with the wolves and behave like wolves, poisoned through and through by the murderous spirit of the world.

When do we make this discovery? In quite ordinary situations in which there does not yet appear to be any scent of murder. *"But if any one has the world's goods, and sees his brother in need, yet closes his heart against him"* (v. 17), that is, who does not do what he gratefully sees the love of God doing, who does not give from his means of subsistence for people in distress, belongs to those who "do not have the love of God remaining in them – to the murderers and the men of death". Who of us does *not* belong there? We rich Christians with the poor Lazarus of the third world before our door, we who deliver arms to the Shah of Persia, we who give money to Somoza and Pinochet, we possessors of shares, of Banks and industrial firms which support the oppressive regime of South Africa, we who long for security, who wish our Government to participate in the deadly armament madness of the whole world, we citizens of Dahlem beside the Turkish children of Kreuzburg who have no future, all we who daily draw our rich incomes at the cost of countless underprivileged people, and require of our politicians that they ensure that our privileges are not taken from us. "No German can say that he is not an exploiter" wrote a Brazilian Bishop recently. What does our Christianity amount to, and what our consolation in the love of God, whom we love *"in word and in speech"* and not *"in deed and in truth"* (v. 18), if it is true that he who does not love, who does not give his life for his brother, remains in death?

Here the love of God that has been a joy to us becomes an accusation. The heart that has been penetrated by the love of God, it is just this heart that condemns us. We are Christians, in so far as our heart condemns us; we are Christians in so far as our heart condemns our actual Christianity. Christians are people who are torn apart by the contradiction of the life which is bestowed upon them, and the death in which they still participate, and who therefore ask in great distress "How does the love of God remain in us?"

The letter of John proposes to make this contradiction visible to us, and to drive us to face this question – not indeed to make us come to grief or fall into despair because we see that true Christianity is much too difficult for us. It is not given to us to make us give up in resignation. We are, let's face it, men of death, murderers just as much as the others, and now we howl as wolves with the wolves. The aim of the letter is to make us long for a better answer, and hear the answer that is given to us here, and let ourselves be helped by it to begin again, and at least in a preliminary manner to come into contradiction with the wolf-world, and to live in the midst of this world of death as men of the love of God. The answer that will help us to do this is a twofold one.

First, in this process of judgement, our heart appears against us like a public prosecutor, with his inexorable charges and condemnations. But God, before whom the trial takes place, is not identical with this prosecutor. The heart – or: the conscience, is not simply as is sometimes said, God's voice; it is our voice, the voice of our hearts touched by God's love. It perceives with horror the contradiction between death and life in our own life. But of God it is said that *"wherever our heart condemns us, God is greater than our hearts, and he knows everything."* (v. 20.) What does that mean? We accuse ourselves, but we also defend ourselves; we point out the fact that our Christianity is not just negligible, but has already produced a few acts of love; that we give to this and give to that, and what we rich Christians do through charitable work, through "Bread for the World" and "Adveniat" and "Misereor" for poor Lazarus. And we plead as mitigating circumstances that we are weak men and not saints, our readiness for sacrifice has after all its limits, and we ought not to overstrain it, and should we not also enjoy God's gifts, should we let every extra purchase and every holiday journey be spoilt by the accusations of our bad conscience? And, in conclusion, the distress in the world is so great, and if our capitalism is to blame for it, it is not the only cause, and we individuals can only give a quite unimportant amount of help to alleviate it.

Answer: you don't need to make any defensive speeches in God's presence. He *"Knows all things"*, he knows how little we give, and knows that we are but dust, he knows everything in our favour, all the mitigating circumstances, and the vastness of the need. And *"he is greater than our heart"*, his love is given to the wolves, the murderers who are the slaves of death, this terrible world, for which he sacrifices himself, and he loves also his weak disciples, his so inadequate co-workers with all their servitude and their relapses into the old way of death. He has known these for long, before our heart recognized them and accused us. His love is understanding and forgiving and untiring, forgiving more than seventy times seven, God's greatness is his never-ceasing forgiveness.

With this, says the writer of the letter, who puts himself wholly on our side, and does not in the least talk down to us, we can *"reassure our hearts"* (v. 19). There is an illegitimate self-reassurance and easement of our minds, when someone wholly represses the accusations of conscience, and continually tries to deceive himself and other people about the excellence of his Christian life. And there is a legitimate reassurance and easement, which we do not administer to ourselves, but which God gives to us with his forgiveness, and gives to us precisely in the moment of truth, where we no longer hold on to our self-deception, but expose ourselves without defence to the charges of our conscience. When we no longer defend and justify ourselves, then God, who is greater than our heart, defends us, and holds us fast as a mother does her little naughty child. *"Little children"* and *"beloved"* therefore is what the author of the letter calls us, and we can breathe again; we are not rejected as we deserve to be, we are still accepted by the love of God.

But that things may not stop here, we go on to the second part of the answer. To the command to believe in this forgiveness of his in Jesus Christ, and to rely on it, there is added the new command to go in mission to our brothers, including the Cain-men around us. *"This is his commandment, that we believe in the name of his Son Jesus Christ, and love one another"* (v. 23). He needs us further, that through us, through our love "in reality and truth", his love may come to the loveless men of death. The reassurance given through forgiveness is not given in order that we may calmly go to sleep. Hans Joachim Iwand once said, "Some Christians, when they hear the word forgiveness, turn themselves over and sleep on, and they then call that conversion". Forgiveness is granted to us, that now, for the first time, we should stir ourselves, no longer reflecting anxiously about our inability to love, no more letting ourselves be.paralysed by the knowledge of our weakness and the immensity of the need around us, but placing anew our life-resources and our privileges in his service. Forgiveness is not a pillow to rest on, but a stimulus. By this it shows that it is not an illegitimate, but a legitimate reassurance. God calms us so that he may at once again disturb us.

Now we begin to take counsel anew what we with our small power can do in the immense distresses of the world, what individuals can do, what the congregation of Dahlem, the Church of West Berlin, the Evangelical Church in Germany can do, what political policy we can support, and what political policy we must oppose. There will on this point repeatedly be differences of opinion, and thus disagreement among us. But if, and in so far as we all accept the principle that nothing that belongs to us belongs to us ourselves, that everything that belongs to us has been requisitioned by the love of God, then we have a common alignment and a common criterion for our deliberations which will certainly from time lead to joint practical action. "What is not service, is robbery", as Martin Luther said unforgettably, and it is just the love of God which invites us no longer to be robbers among robbers, but co-workers with love. When we remain, in however weak and untutored a way, in loving action, not merely talking about love, then the love of God abides in us and we abide in it.

In a new novel of the Swedish poet Lars Gustafson "The Death of a Beekeeper", (1978), stands the sentence "If one says 'I love you', there is only one possibility, that one does it". That is the movement into which this text together with the whole Gospel, seeks to attract us and drive us. Instead of the way of death it is the way of life.

The Universality of Jesus Christ

In many and various ways God spoke of old to our fathers by the prophets; but in these last days he has spoken to us by a Son, whom he appointed the heir of all things, through whom also he created the world. He reflects the glory of God and bears the very stamp of his nature, upholding the universe by his word of power. When he had made purification for sins, he sat down at the right hand of the Majesty on high. Hebrews 1, 1.

This splendid beginning of the Letter to the Hebrews is in Greek a single sentence of such wonderful construction that it rejoices the heart of everyone that knows it. It is magnificent by reason of its outreach into all times and places of the universe. Perhaps the best way to unravel its meaning is to ask, what difference does it make to us if this is literally true? We ourselves are mentioned in this sentence *"he has in these last days spoken to us"*. This "us" is so universal that no one should regard himself as excluded or not intended. We do not belong to the *"fathers to whom God of old spoke in many and various ways by the prophets"*, that is, we certainly do not belong to the people of Israel. But this precisely is the event of which the whole New Testament speaks, and that is the fulfilment of what *"of old"* had been audible only to the narrow circle of hearers, to Israel. Now, with the event whose beginning and significance is brought before us at Christmas, the door opens to the whole world, and everyone, absolutely everyone, belongs to the circle of hearers, together with Israel. This one Jew, Jesus of Nazareth, is the Word of God to Israel, *and* to everyone. How are we involved by this, what is then our true situation? In five points we are given an answer by the primitive Christian witness, who is otherwise unknown to us, who wrote the Letter to the Hebrews.

1. *He has spoken to us.* We know already how important it is that we should be spoken to. If no one had ever spoken to us, we would have not become human, probably we would not have survived the age of infancy. We have become human by the fact that people have spoken human words to us. And the words that we hear from Jesus and the Prophets are human words. But the special thing about the speaking of the true Prophets, together with Jesus, is, that in them and through them another voice than the voice of us men is audible. In a word, that which hitherto was dumb, speaks to us. Apart from the speech of man, everything around us, beasts, plants, and stones, the world of nature and the universe that surrounds us, is dumb. Let us be clear about this: we exist in the midst of an immense silence. And behind this silent universe, behind everything that is and lives, there stretches the eternal silence, destiny, which neither speaks nor can be spoken to, and which rules over gods and men and everything that is. Many people, who today use the word "God", mean nothing but this. They speak of "mystery", and mean by that this impenetrable silence, which gives us

no answer whether we address our questions to its dumbness in hope or in fear. But now, where hitherto there was silence, someone is speaking to us. Out of the stillness comes a voice; we can hear it, we can answer it. The final truth behind all the stars and the gods is not this deadly silence, this all-devouring dumb eternity into which each of us appears to sink when he dies. The final truth and reality is a living voice which comes down to us, on this dust-particle of earth, and seeks you and me, the insects of a day. It makes itself heard now in human speech, in order that we may know whence we come, and whither we are going, and "what shall for ever stand/When all things earthly blow away/Away like dust and sand". To us, to each one of us, human words are spoken out of eternity.

2. What here speaks to us, or, better, *he who here speaks to us is real, eternal love*. As this voice spoke to Israel in the prophets, Israel at once knew "Behind it there is nothing higher, this is not merely provisional truth; this is final truth". But because this voice, as it does with us too, speaks in a friendly and stern manner, because it gives promises and commands, Gospel and law, we may well ask, "Who is this that speaks to us here in his heart of hearts?" In Jesus this becomes clear; in Jesus – this is what the word *"Son"* means – the eternal Voice has spoken, the eternal God has opened his heart. Jesus is the revelation of the divine heart, and this heart is love – a word which is today as much abused as the word "God" and the word "Christmas". So that we must first recover its full power and significance. "God is a fiery furnace full of love" says Luther somewhere. This is wonderful, it is anything but self-evident; it is an unbelievable fact. Of this the phenomenon of Jesus should make us sure, to hear him, to cling to him, to follow after him in his way, to hope in him – that unites us with God's love, that will make us certain that this love is the final truth and reality. He, Jesus, *"reflects the glory of God and bears the very stamp of his nature"*.

3. If the eternal God shows himself here below among us as our brother and friend, and speaks to us, this means also that our *relation to this world* in which we live, is changed. A gigantic universe, flying asunder since the primal explosion, subject to its own laws, endless empty space, galaxies coming into being and passing away, and ourselves, insignificant microbes in the midst of it all – what is the sense, what is the meaning of this? Luther says in his Christmas hymn that the coming of Jesus "gives the world a new splendour". In this new splendour fundamental questions are given a reassuring answer. "To whom does all this belong?" "To the Son, in whom God opens his heart to us." "Whence did it come?" "From the heart of God, which is love, and which discloses itself in Jesus." "Where is it all going?" "Not into nothingness, but towards him. He is the goal." *"Whom he appointed the heir of all things, through whom also he created the world; he upholds the universe by the word of his power."* If before, we were forsaken insignificant beings in an indifferent universe, now we are in a world that comes out of the love of God, a world irradiated by that love. In his eyes there is no difference between great and small,

countless galaxies of immeasurable extension, and the smallest midge, to all he is equally near, all belong to him.

But this also means that the world does not belong to us. As modern man felt the universe to be infinite empty space, Godforsaken like himself, he began to think of the nature of the earth, the nearest point of the world to him, and of everything else that he can today reach from the earth, as nothing but material which he can exploit for his purposes and destroy. Today we see the desolation which we have caused by this, and continue to cause, as the greatest threat to humanity. Our godless treatment of nature, which is unknown to the so-called "nature peoples" whom we civilized races are accustomed in our arrogance to despise, will be the ruin of us if we do not make a radical change. In order to indicate the theme of this change it is only necessary to mention the word plutonium, which was very unfortunately dealt with in the past week in our Federal Parliament, the word plutonium – the worst conceivable poison, of which a small quantity is sufficient to destroy us all, of which we yearly produce thousands of tons, a poison which God has not created, but which we have created and which, in more than ten thousand years, if there are still men on the earth, will be the only legacy which we leave to these late descendants. The only answer that we can give to them, namely that in a shortage of energy we were not willing to do without this energy, will certainly not serve us for an excuse. Either plutonium – or nature as the property of Jesus, the heir to the universe, that is the hard alternative of death and life which we confront today.

4. After speaking of God's voice in the Prophets and Jesus, and of the "new splendour" which the world receives thereby, it is we who become the theme, we men. What is to be said about us today without this Jesus? The Bible has a word about our present situation, a very much abused and at the same time very relevant word, the word sin. We are dying in our sin, our godless destruction of nature, the godless class struggle of the rich peoples against the poor. But that is only the reflection on a big scale of what is always happening among us on a small scale, our lovelessness, our hardness of hearing when God calls to us, and also the shocking perversion today of our Christmas gift-giving into a consumers' bonanza – we must see all these things together when we hear the word sin. In Jesus God opens his heart to us, to us men who are dying in our sin. *"He has made purification for sins."* Purification for sins, that means, what was hopelessly old and beyond change, can become new. That means, where you previously thought "I can never get free of what I have done", that the burden that stifles you is taken away and put into the past, so that it can no longer obstruct the future. Where you thought, "That's how I am, no one can change me any more", a new life is set before you instead of the old life, a life with new possibilities. Where in bitterness you see other men as irretrievably wicked, now you shall see the living God at work, who has opened his heart in Jesus to set free those people of whom you think so reproachfully from the morass of evil into which they have strayed.

THE UNIVERSALITY OF JESUS CHRIST

"Purification from sin" means lastly also that in the fight against evil in
us and in others, you are not fighting alone, where your power, as you
must repeatedly see, achieves nothing, but with you is he who bears all
things by his word of power. No victory is promised to us in the fight
against evil, but he will be victorious.

5. And all this, not only temporarily, for the few years until we are
laid in the grave. The good that we experience here from this Jesus and
his Gospel is not everything. On the contrary, it is only the beginning.
It goes further, it does not return again at last and meaninglessly to the
grave. It is not cancelled out by death, it goes onwards and upwards. In
the picture-language of our text, *"he has sat down at the right hand of
the Majesty on high"*. He who purifies us, who brings us out of the
ruined life into a life that has a future. He, in whom on earth the
splendour of the love of God has come to shine inextinguishably. He –
and with him, we also, "Jesus lives, our hearts know well. Naught from
him our love shall sever." Everything in the world is transitory, this
Jesus is ultimate. To be united with him means to be united with the
ultimate truth, with the ultimate reality, with the love of God, from
which we came, and to which we are going. That is the Christmas
message of the Letter to the Hebrews. From the stable at Bethlehem it
looks out to the distance and up to the heights, into infinite dimensions
that are too distant for our conceiving, and everyone may easily say;
"That is too high for me, and too difficult, must I believe all that?" You
must not believe anything. It was a great mistake in the Christian
Church that people frequently attached "must" to statements of faith;
if you don't believe that, you won't be saved, you will be rejected by
God. This was a complete misunderstanding of the heart of the Christian message. The words "faith" and "must" don't belong together at
all. There is no "you must". But our question perhaps means something quite different. Perhaps it means "May I believe that? It is not
only too high for my understanding, it is even further from my experience, my day to day experience is different from this description of it. I
do not hear God speaking to me, I do not see the universe penetrated
and carried by the love of God, I feel my age and not these new
possibilities. May I believe something so unbelievable? May I rely on
it? May I dare to live with it and follow this Jesus, cost what it may?"

With this question let us now listen to the Christmas message. The
best that this listening can do is to help us again to take a few steps in
this direction. Probably no one will be able to appropriate wholly these
immeasurably great words. Everyone at first lays hold of a fringe of
them. One takes Jesus as an example for his life, another is encouraged
by Jesus to stand up more adventurously for justice and peace against
all wrong and hatred; another experiences something of forgiveness,
and thereby becomes himself a man who forgives, another is helped by
this encouragement in his fear of life, and yet another receives from it
new power to be in his situation of conflict a uniting reconciling person;
yet another allows the name of Jesus in his last grave illness to take
away the fear of dying. Each one lays hold of a fringe, and is then led

ever further into ever new discoveries, ever wider horizons, to ever greater splendid knowledge, until we finally shall see all this "face to face".

Look Forward!

*After this I saw four angels standing at the four corners of the earth,
holding back the four winds of the earth, so that no wind might blow on
earth or sea or against any tree. Then I saw another angel ascend from
the rising of the sun, with the seal of the living God, and he called with a
loud voice to the four angels who had been given power to harm earth
and sea, saying, "Do not harm the earth or the sea or the trees, till we
have sealed the servants of our God upon their foreheads". And I heard
the number of the sealed, a hundred and forty-four thousand sealed, out
of every tribe of the sons of Israel, twelve thousand sealed out of the tribe
of Judah, twelve thousand of the tribe of Reuben, twelve thousand of the
tribe of Gad, twelve thousand of the tribe of Asher, twelve thousand of
the tribe of Naphtali, twelve thousand of the tribe of Manasseh, twelve
thousand of the tribe of Simeon, twelve thousand of the tribe of Levi,
twelve thousand of the tribe of Issachar, twelve thousand of the tribe of
Zebulun, twelve thousand of the tribe of Joseph, twelve thousand sealed
out of the tribe of Benjamin.*

*After this I looked, and behold a great multitude which no man could
number, from every nation, from all tribes and peoples and tongues,
standing before the throne and before the Lamb, clothed in white robes,
with palm branches in their hand, and crying out with a loud voice,
"Salvation belongs to our God who sits upon the throne, and to the
Lamb!" And all the angels stood round the throne and round the elders
and the four living creatures, and they fell upon their faces before the
throne and worshipped God, saying "Amen! Blessing and glory and
wisdom and thanksgiving and honour and power and might be to our
God for ever and ever! Amen".*

*Then one of the elders addressed me, saying, "Who are these, clothed
in white robes, and whence have they come?" I said to him, "Sir, you
know". And he said to me, "These are they who have come out of the
great tribulation; they have washed their robes and made them white in
the blood of the Lamb. Therefore are they before the throne of God, and
serve him day and night within his temple; and he who sits upon the
throne will shelter them with his presence. They shall hunger no more,
neither thirst any more; the sun shall not strike them, nor any scorching
heat. For the Lamb in the midst of the throne will be their shepherd, and
he will guide them to springs of living water; and God will wipe away
every tear from their eyes."* Revelation, 7.

Whether this text now seems strange or comforting to us, or sets our
imagination in motion – it will become important to us the more we
make it clear to ourselves that it expresses in the form of a vision what
is the content of the whole Gospel. The whole Gospel calls to us "look
forward!" however things are going with you. Look forward! Hope will
come to you from that direction, and staying power. Look forward, you
see there what gives you the power to hold on! Accordingly, number-

less Christians have looked forward, and thus looking forward, have died. And accordingly, many other people also have looked forward in the hope that this better future could somehow lie within history, and that in the course of evolution we would reach it through our progress, and they have therefore fought for progress, and staked their lives upon it. Today in the case of many people this hopeful expectation of progress has been paralysed. A poll taken recently has shown that, in contrast with earlier times, less than half of the citizens of the Federal Republic believe in the progress of humanity. But this means that they do not expect for themselves anything better, but rather something worse, and they have also their reasons for doing so, and for that reason they prefer not to look forward, but concern themselves only with the present, seeing before them only the approach of age and death, and therefore live rather gloomily a day at a time.

But the Bible does not cease to call continually to us, dejected and anxious about the future as we are, "Look forward!" For this reason this text is set for the end of the Church year just as the Revelation of John stands at the end of the New Testament, and at the end of the whole Bible, in order to tell us: in everything that is here said to you of consolation and guidance to help you in your earthly life, in all this you must keep looking forward, for only then will everything have its real meaning, basis, and logical connection.

That quickly becomes clear to us when we see to what group in particular this call is directed. The people who are here spoken to are those who have *"Come out of great tribulation"*. So the people principally aimed at are those who are now in great tribulation, who now do not know where to turn, surrounded on every side by night and death and anxiety. In this remarkable book of the Revelation of John, which does not at all believe in progress, but which sees mankind advancing into great terrors, and for that reason is called the most relevant book of the Bible by some clearsighted monitors of our time, in this book, before our chapter, the four apocalyptic riders, war, civil war, natural disturbance and nation-wide death (at that time people thought of plague, today we might add to it radioactivity!) are let loose on the earth, and after our chapter there sound the six trumpets of woe. But in the middle, in between these proclamations of terror, this call "You who are in great tribulation, look forward! There you will see, with the help of this prophetic vision, what gives you the power now to endure the great tribulation." To endure – that meant for the first readers of this book, for the little, slandered, oppressed, persecuted martyr churches of early Christianity; not to throw away their new-found faith, the transformation of their lives, the discipleship of Jesus, their nonconformity, not to give up their non-cooperation with what everybody is doing, even when prison and death are the price, to remain witnesses to life, even if witnesses condemned to death in the midst of a society in fact condemned to death because it promised life to itself from the production of death and methods of death.

To endure means also for us today, to remain in the movement into which the Gospel has brought us, in the service of Jesus rather than in the service of money, of career, of increased consumption, in not going along with the worship of Mammon, with the general cowardice, with resignation, in joyful hearing of the promise of faith, in standing up for the victims of violence and exploitation. But for this to be not a mere gloomy endurance that in the end falls into resignation, but a meaningful endurance that in spite of all reverses is borne up by hope, we need a vision of the goal, and a certainty of reaching it. For this reason the Gospel calls to us "Look forward!" – and for this reason the Revelation of John brings into the announcement of terrors the vision of men who have attained the goal, the redeemed, gathered round God and the Lamb, with suffering behind them, now in eternal joy, seeing God, with all their tears dried, all questions stilled, with the springs of life in ceaseless thanks and praise. Let me draw two things here to your attention:

1. *God and the Lamb* are the centre, the ground of joy, and in our looking forward the ground of hope. Not a God without the Lamb, that would be a God who sits in state above us, unmoved and untouched by our suffering, an inscrutable Providence, an indecipherable fate – how could we thank him? God *and* the Lamb – that is the God, who himself in Jesus Christ has shared in our sorrows, has wholly sacrificed himself for us, who knows exactly what we are going through, why we cry out and accuse him, who himself in his own person has known the God-forsakenness of the torture-chambers and terrible deathbeds, a brother among brothers. And God and the Lamb – that is the God who in the resurrection of our crucified brother Jesus has promised and proclaimed to us all the victory of life over death, in order that we may be able to look up to it in the midst of night as to the goal destined for us, to the hope promised to us, which nothing can wrest from us, which neither age nor death nor all the torturers and murderers can shut off from us. The prospect of this goal and the presence of this brotherly God who has pity on us and suffers for us, and the presence of his Spirit who helps us through, that is the power which enables us to endure, which helps us to have faith when everything around us and in us is set to make faith and hope impossible for us.

Thus it is faith that has the last word, not what reason and probability say to us. Reason and probability say to us often enough that all is lost and in vain. In faith, that is, in hearing the promise that is contained in this vision, and in the confidence which is continually reawakened by this hearing, we set against it; Nothing is lost, nothing is in vain. Tribulation is not the last thing, joy, arrival at the goal will be the last thing, and for this reason we shall be able to hold on in faith and in hope, hearing the promise ever anew.

2. There are two different groups of men whom we see arriving at the goal, the 144,000 from all the tribes of Israel, and the innumerable company from all the peoples of the earth. In these days especially we are thinking of those who have been persecuted, tortured and murdered in the people of Israel, of the people of Israel, now that forty

years have passed since the first climax of the persecution of Jews in our land, which was followed by the great murder of the war years. It was now upon them that the great affliction came, not upon us, us Aryan Germans, many of whom took part in most various ways, and if they did not take part, they looked on, and if they did not look on, then they looked away because they did not want to know anything about it, and in so far as we knew, and tried to help, we still always had it much better than those whom we helped, and all the sufferings which then as God's judgement came through the war on our guilty people, were not so terrible as what these Jews suffered from people of our own nation and by the toleration of our nation.

Of the Jews many went praying into the gas-chambers. Many died in despair with the accusations of Job against the God of Israel. All of them, the whole of Israel, with all the victims of the Pogroms which through the centuries were organized in the part of the so-called Christian peoples, are there represented by the 144,000 sealed men before the throne of God and the Lamb, who, let us remember, was one of them. For this number is not a limited number, but a symbolic number. Twelve is the number of fullness, and twelve times twelve thousand means the entire fullness of Israel. We cannot see the meaning of the guidance of God, who is the God of Abraham, Isaac and Jacob, and yet deals so hardly with his people, so hardly as he dealt with himself in his Son Jesus Christ. This people is a people of the Cross more than the Church which calls itself a Church of the Cross. We see it there, arrived at the goal, the un-lost people, preserved through all its sufferings. Only together with this people shall we see ourselves there at the goal. And brotherliness to Israel, and therefore deep penitence for our guilt against Israel, must now be a mark of the Christian Church without which we cannot be the Church of Christ, the Jew from Israel.

The other group round the throne of God and the Lamb, with palms in their hands – and palm branches were then not only the sign of peace, but above all signs of victory, to be carried at victory-festivals! – are the respresentatives of the whole of mankind, who are the objects of the love of God and the Lamb. But by whom are we represented there? By those who have *"come out of great tribulation"*. People with bloodstained clothing, bloody not with the blood of their enemies, but with their own blood, from the wounds with which they have been wounded. It is not said whether here we are to think only of Christian martyrs. They are victims *"from all nations, races, peoples and languages"*, downtrodden people, members of fringe-groups, martyrs for human rights, of whom especially our century is full. The other day Ernesto Cardenal the poet-priest, reported of a young fisherman from his group in Solentiname in Nicaragua, to which we owe the rousing conversations about the Gospel; (Ernesto Cardenal: Das Evangelium der Bauern von Solentiname, Wuppertal 1976.) That the young man was dragged off by Somoza's National Guard, and sent a message now by an escaped fellow-prisoner: he lies in a wet, dark hole of a prison, they have broken all his fingers, and if he happens to come out again alive, he will all his life long be a cripple and incapable of work, a victim of the tyrant, with whom big industrial firms of our land maintain friendly relations. These sacrifices, the sacrifices also of our politics and our exploitation of the Third World, represent us there above, and without a great judgement, without great remorse and shame, without pleading for forgiveness, if they receive us there, we shall not be accepted. For this vision does not really speak of us as we sit here. We have many a burden in life to carry, but the great affliction of the Jews has not come upon us, and we have quickly left behind us the ravages of the war, partly through participation in a world economic system that secures for us prosperity, and hunger and tyranny for many millions. Nor does being Christian bring us any tribulation in our land, on the contrary it brings advantages so long as we do not really and in practice become followers of Christ, and show ourselves by our actions to be the brothers of those who are thrust into the affliction of hunger and oppression. But then, when through our brotherliness we have come near to them, then we too shall be assailed by the despair to which they are exposed in their miserable prisons. Then we shall ask with them, "Where is God?" and with them groan "My God, my God, why hast thou forsaken me?" For such an hour the promise of this vision is given to us with them. Some of us have known how in such a situation and in such hours this is no mere empty word, as it well might appear to spectators outside the affliction, but a life-giving influx of power, no mere consolation for the hereafter, but comfort from beyond, giving power for this world.

There the bloodstained garments are washed in another's blood, in the blood of our brother, the Lamb, who died for us. There what was sinful is washed away, that is, what was against God even in our best struggles, and also in the manner in which we fought, and the blood of suffering is washed away, the battle has been won, we are through! The white garments are the garments of the feast of victory. The cries, the complaints, and the questions have fallen silent. "In that day you will ask me no questions" (John 16, 23). Thankfulness and praise have the last word. Do not entangle yourselves in speculative questions, why God beforehand permitted these afflictions, and how is it with life after death, what does it look like, and how is it possible! believe that this promise is true – and you will find how necessary and how helpful it is if we are to come through all afflictions in faith and in hope!

If possible, so far as it depends on you, live peaceably with all.
Romans 12, 18.

Dear friends! You in any case! You in every case! if these words are for
anyone, then for you! And if for no one else, then still for you! Peace
should find its first vanguard and last refuge with you. A nucleus of
peace, an atomic core of peace in society, that is what the Christian
congregation should be. It should cooperate everywhere where people
are concerned about peace. It should not collaborate, it should everywhere be a centre of resistance where a society becomes militarist,
brutalized and fascistic. Your message is a message of peace; the God
whom you are privileged to know, and of whom you ought to be
speaking to all other men, is the God of peace; your Saviour who
wishes to heal your life, bringing it to soundness and freedom, is called
the Prince of Peace, the Spirit with which he wishes to pervade the
world, is a Spirit of peace. Summary of all this for you, for your life in
the midst of other people: *"If possible, so far as it depends on you, live
peaceably with all men."*
    Anyone who has even a slight knowledge of Jesus, of the content of
the Gospel, might think that that was so self-evident, that this little
sentence of Paul was quite enough, and that no further word is necessary. Message and behaviour, faith and life must after all agree. But in
the history of Christendom there is often a wide gap between them.
Pierre Bayle, a cynical philosopher, wrote some two hundred years
ago, In waging war, "even the Turks must yield precedence to the
Christians. Indeed, a great honour for the Christians, that they are
greater masters of the art of killing, bombarding, and extirpating the
human race than the Mohammedans." When you ask what sort of
people have brought it about that we have come to such a point in the
extirpation of the human race, that the survival of the whole of humanity stands in question, then among the many names of scientists,
technicians and politicians who had a share in it, you will find compara-
tively few names of non-Christians. Obviously the Church which in
Baptism has made them members of the Body of the Prince of Peace,
has not up to date opposed them with great passion. "Leave off from
this devil's work! You can't at the same time be Christians and invent
these devilries, produce them and use them as political means, and
finally, as means of war!" Some thirty million men today work on
armaments, about twenty million are under arms, over four hundred
thousand scientists and technicians are active in the laboratories of the
armament industry, millions of them are baptized persons. What the
great Churches of Christendom have said on this up to date, largely
limited itself to the platitude that everyone must decide according to
his own conscience, but gave no clear instruction to this conscience, did
not confront this conscience with the clear challange "Away with this
devilry!"
    That is a great tragedy of our century. In 1958 there was talk of a
strike of Christians against atomic weapons, and a Synod of the

Evangelical Church in Germany had a consultation about it – without result. In the sixties the Second Vatican Council had a consultation about it, but all the clearcut proposals which were put forward there, were left on the table.

Today, when the complete annihilation of our land threatens, above all youth groups carry the motto "Create peace without arms" through the land. But still this has not become the general watchword of the Christian Churches, never yet taken up by their official organs, by our Synods, by the Pope with full clarity. Still the evangelical circles, which boast themselves of special loyalty to the faith, stand on one side, and consider that as an earthly question which does not concern Christians. But here Paul says quite clearly that one cannot have peace with God without creating peace among men. And of course that cannot apply merely to our behaviour to our nearest neighbours, with whom we have to do immediately. It concerns equally our political behaviour in which we all participate. For it is in the name of all of us that today our countries go on arming and arming and arming, and it is asserted that this is in our defence, and apparently, so long as we do not protest, it is being done with our assent.

Is it really being done with our assent? Do we wish this protection? Do we wish that in a first strike or in a second strike the towns of the Soviet Union with all their hundreds of thousands of people should be obliterated, in order that we may continue to enjoy prosperity, free market economy, and democratic freedoms? Do we wish that? That is the first question to every one of us, and to the Christian Church. From this arises at once a second question. Are we seeking with all our might a way out, by means of which the threat of mutual annihilation may be removed, by means of which we may at least live side by side in peace with the peoples of the east as well as with the peoples of the west? Have we realized with Gustav Heinemann that today peace is the question of supreme importance, for which we must venture everything? Or do we still hold with Walter Scheel his successor, that war is the issue of supreme importance, for which our Federal Army and all of us must be prepared? When the recruits took their oath last week, did anyone say to them what their promise "To serve truly the Federal Republic of Germany" really meant? They promised in the ultimate event of war not to fire a shot, because every shot will be a shot against the Fatherland, and not for the Fatherland, a contribution to the annihilation of the Fatherland, not a contribution to its preservation? The Christian community among us allowed the Chorale "I pray the power of love" to be played while the oath was being taken. Do we wish that in the ultimate issue of war our soldiers should do what this Chorale says: "I wish, instead of thinking of myself, (which means; instead of destroying others to protect my own interests) to sink myself in the sea of love". If we don't wish that, then in this week when the command was given "Caps off for prayer!" many blasphemies went up to heaven.

We see that we are pressed very hard by this simple sentence of the

Apostle. Obviously as it may follow from all that the Gospel says, it leads us into great difficulties. Even in private life it is a great demand in marital and family disputes, among relatives and friends, at our place of work and in our neighbourhood, in the conflicts of interests, and not least often in our church congregations; to be always intent on understanding the other man, always to see things from the other man's point of view – always to put oneself in his situation, and to think responsibly for him and not against him, always to be the first to seek for a peaceful solution, not to take things ill, not to bear grudges, not to create a hostile image, again and again to give up our rights for the sake of peace. From men whose interests centre in themselves, to make us people whose whole concern is for other people – that is the great concern of Jesus, that is the great change that God wants to bring through the Gospel into our way of life.

In order to escape from the difficulty, someone might now say "You have overlooked the reservation with which Paul begins. He says indeed *"If it is possible,* keep peace with everyone". So it all depends on the other man. "Even the best man cannot live in peace. When wicked neighbours will not let him be." When your neighbour won't cooperate, then you can't! When in spite of all my offers of peace, he strikes the first blow, then, though I regret it, I must hit back – and for this, I also must be armed. This interpretation of his words, which has repeatedly been given, would have brought Paul to his feet in anger. "Tit for tat" – God did not need to become a man and go to the Cross in order to give us this rule for life. In order to free us from this rule of so-called prudence, this so-called justice, God himself renounced this rule. He did not respond to our enmity against him with a like enmity on his part against us, but gave his life for his enemies, and thereby showed us the way of another righteousness, a new righteousness. Paul's word *"if it be possible"* is not meant to open again to us the old way of "tit for tat". That is now closed behind us. "If it is possible" – that only means: you have not the other man in your power, you can – it is to be hoped! – influence him by your readiness for peace, but you cannot compel him. As far as he is concerned, he can always hit out at you. But as far as you are concerned, you as a man of peace must always keep yourself ready for peace, time and again, striving to reach a peaceful relationship between yourself and the other man, and do all that you can to ensure that you live together in harmony instead of conflict. Note well: Paul is not here giving us a rule of thumb that could mechanically be applied in all cases. He is indicating a way of behaviour which has its origin in God's rejection of violence, and his love for his enemies. To be more concerned for others than for one's own life – that is the guiding principle, the new, better righteousness. That is how God deals with us, and that is how we ought to deal with one another, set free from the old compulsive rule of "tit for tat".

To put this into practice requires the complete commitment of our faith just as it does the complete commitment of our understanding. Into what difficulties Jesus Christ's mission of peace brings us, we see clearly as soon as we realize that those about whom we should be concerned, are the same people from whom we must protect ourselves, and those from whom we must protect ourselves now become those for whom we must be concerned. Human life cannot exist except under the conditions that men protect themselves, and must protect themselves against men – through law, justice, police, and so on. So long as all of us together are sinful human beings, that is necessary; even the Gospel does not wish to cancel that out. And by doing so we do no injustice even to those from whose unjust intentions we protect ourselves. They too live under the protection of law, with which we protect ourselves against them, and them against us. But even in criminal law, for example, it will be decisive whether we merely wish to protect ourselves against others, or whether we are also concerned about these others, the law-breakers. In this matter today in our criminal law and in our penal system we are only making a first beginning. Our prisons must be much more changed, they must not be penal institutions, but real institutions of re-socialization, if we are really filled with concern about those against whom we protect ourselves. Only then would we inquire more than we have done hitherto, as to what must be changed in our society in order that people do not in such large numbers require punishment, inquiring also how far society – and that includes us ourselves, who live from the advantages of our society, produces these people who commit punishable offences. In the life of the nations too, we protect ourselves from one another. So long as all States do not come under a strong international law and strong institutions administering international law, we are living in the barbaric age of the mailed fist, and cannot stop the States from protecting themselves against each other by armaments. In the Movement "Living without Armaments" many of us, I among others, have signed a declaration that we personally, in the obedience and confidence of faith, are ready to live without military protection, and even more so without today's weapons of annihilation. But this does not at once mean an answer to all the questions of our political responsibility. "To make peace without arms" does not simply mean, "Lay down your arms!" But this motto calls us away from the illusion that ever more armament means ever more security. Its intention is to remind us that for long the situation has been such that the ever greater armament means ever greater insecurity, indeed, as the American sociologist C. Wright Mills said in the fifties, the chief reason for the Third World War would foreseeably be the present state of armaments. Its intention is that the armaments race be replaced by negotiations, and that in the place of the bogus negotiations we have had hitherto, there should be genuine negotiations, that offensive weapons should be reduced in favour of weapons of defence, that atomic weapons should be destroyed, that we may be ready to take "measures creative of trust" as the expression of the peace-investigators has it, and also to take unilateral measures which convince the other side of our willingness to disarm, and that we take seriously the Soviet Union's interest in peace.

This must proceed from the knowledge that there are no longer reasons which can make war a conceivable possibility, for there is no longer any reason that can oblige us or cause us to wish to seek our mutual destruction, and from this it follows that there are only reasons for peace. Our armaments have long since overstepped the boundary where they serve the preservation of peace and justice. Our armaments are killing us already, before war starts. Instead of armament must come disarmament; that is today the most important interest of humanity.

To these great tasks the message of peace of the Gospel extends today. "Peace has no lobby among us" wrote Dorothee Sölle some years ago. Paul asks us if that is now to be changed. "Be, inasmuch as in you lies, a lobby for peace!" that is how one can translate his word. For this reason we may no longer leave the questions of armaments to the experts, we must ourselves create an opinion where armaments are a danger to peace, we msut not see the world only from a western, but from an eastern perspective, and be friends with the Russians as with the Americans, concerned as much for the Russians as for ourselves. Much more would have to be added, we have much in this lobby to discuss and to do. I add here only one concrete statement, in order to clarify my meaning. If in three years four hundred middle-range rockets are sited in West Germany, then we have come a great deal nearer to our annihilation.

"If possible": in this there is an advantage for us. For that means that what we now have to do, and will do, is not dependent on our success in doing so, on our really preventing war and annihilation. We must do it in any case, and in any case it is meaningful to do this. We are dependent only on the call and mission of our Lord, who says; "I call you in any case and equip you as a lobby for peace." Therefore we pray you, our Lord Jesus Christ, make us men of peace in a sense quite different from what we have been hitherto, and in addition give blessing and success to the protection of our human race which is today so imperilled by our armaments.

AMEN.

The fear of the Lord is a fountain of life, that one may avoid the snares of death. Proverbs 14, 27.

In the narratives of the birth of Jesus, there occurs very often the word "fear", for they are pervaded by the comforting, strengthening call "Fear not!" "Joseph, son of David, fear not ..." (Matthew 1, 20). "Do not be afraid, Mary" (Luke 1, 30). "Be not afraid, for, behold I bring you good news of a great joy" (Luke 2, 10). For this reason the motto chosen for the German Evangelical Kirchentag next June, is "Be not afraid" – urgently necessary in a time in which every morning the opening of a newspaper brings fear to our hearts. The future grows more and more alarming, the world appears to us less and less a world in which one can live. What this growth of apprehension, this increasing fear in the souls of countless people, especially young people, is doing, is evident to all of us. How much the world has changed for the worse in this year 1980, since a few years ago the pollsters could speak of the citizens of our Federation as being fairly content with their situation! In these last days a lawyer in this city made this clear to me, by telling me that twenty years ago he had to take part in the committal of a suicidal woman to a mental hospital. In the psychiatric report it was stated, as a sign of the mental disturbance of this woman that she was haunted by the fear of a third World War. If this is a sign of mental disturbance, then today we would all have to go into a psychiatric clinic – perhaps when we read in the newspapers the headline "In the U.S.A. preparedness to strike the first blow is growing". (Frankfurter Rundschau 10.12.80.) This means that in the most powerful place in the world there are people today for whom it is not inconceivable political action to burn alive hundreds of thousands of Soviet children through an atomic attack on the Soviet Union. Mankind has come to the barbaric age of its history. Everything calls to us today, "Be afraid!" How can the call "Fear not!" make headway against it?

And take this into account also, the places where the Bible itself teaches us to fear. Some time ago, Ernst Käsemann the well-known New Testament scholar in Tübingen said to me that at the Kirchentag people would have to remember that the Bible at least as often says "Be afraid!" That is right. As the shepherds of Bethlehem saw the heavenly glory streaming over them, "they were filled with fear" (Luke 2, 9). And of the women who heard the message of the Resurrection at the grave of Jesus, we are told that "trembling and astonishment had come upon them, and they said nothing to anyone, for they were afraid" (Mark 16, 8). John the Baptist, whom the Church is accustomed to remember on the third Sunday in Advent, frightened the people by a message of fear in face of the coming Judgement. Thus in the Bible, in contrast with a call and summons to fearlessness, there is a call and summons to fear, both together, and related to each other, neither without the other, and both of them immensely important and able to prevent us in these alarming times from falling a victim to fear. Let us speak first of the fearlessness which is commended to us! Who is

it that says to us "Fear not!" Not an agreeable man, who kindly wishes
to calm us. Not politicians and governments, which advise us to have
"courage for the future", and which are yet, as I would like to think,
deeply disquieted by the ever-increasing danger of war, in consequence of the continually increasing armaments.

"Fear not", says the living God to the anxious heart of everyone of
us. He is the source of our life, to whom we owe so many good days; at
our baptism he declared that you and I were his children, and has
caused the message of his love to be brought to us all our life long. We
have heard it so often, gratefully, often with new trust, with little faith,
with unbelief and indifference often enough. Now things are serious,
serious for our hearing, serious also for this God of love. That he
remains true to us, that we remain true to him – everything depends on
that, everything, so that we can hold our heads high, laugh, and hope,
so that we do not collapse, today because of fear, and tomorrow
because of what the future can bring; so that we remain human, so that
our life may not become inhuman, one way or another, despairing or
brutal. The same times which call to us "Be afraid!" call to us also "If
there is one who can help you to overcome fear, then run to him, then
your life is saved, then all things must work together for you, then you
are not lost". I, a trembling man, hear the promise "I am with you, be
not afraid". Hearing this promise I lift up my eyes and see the eternal
love holding me fast by the hand, it surrounds me on all sides, nothing
can happen to me but what you have chosen. You will not forsake me
nor leave me. From you I receive every day food and drink and all that
is necessary for my life. You give me people who through their love
make your love visible to me. You are with me, even if some day you
should take all that from me. You are with me on every bad day as on
every good day. In Jesus you have already laid yourself in my grave.
You lay me in the grave, and you receive me in the grave, and you will
lead me through the gates of death nowhere else but to yourself, and
even if I feel nothing of your power you will still bring me to the goal,
even through the night. Relying on your word, I repeat that every day,
and hold it up against the demons of fear and the news in the papers,
and raise my head again and come out of the egoism of fear, which
makes me think only of myself, and turn again in love to other people,
those most near and those most distant, and take up again the fight of
David against the Goliath of war-armament, and for the preservation of
threatened peace. And even when I do not understand many things
about you, the living God of love, especially not why you permit men in
their darkness so to torment themselves and destroy themselves, and
why your judgements on the peoples are so terrible and strike the
innocent with the guilty – through your concealment you speak to me,
little as I am, and I know that you love all those around me as you love
me, and that you send me to them as a messenger of your love. So,
strengthened by the word of your love, I shall no longer be a slave of my
fear, but only a servant of your love.

That is not impossible; that becomes possible and real now. This can

and shall happen to every one of us anew each day, so that as the
advent song of praise of Zacharias says "We, being delivered out of the
hand of our enemies, (and what is the hand of our enemies with which
they reach out to us, but the fear of them in our hearts!) may serve him
without fear all our days" (Luke 1, 74). The Gospel saves from fear –
and there was never a time in human history in which this salvation was
so necessary as this, and in which mankind had such need of men thus
saved, radiating fearlessness in their midst.

How, in addition to this fearlessnesss enjoined upon us for our
salvation and made possible, is there also a fear enjoined upon us, and
what have the two to do with one another? The Gospel sees as the chief
danger and affliction of our lives the faithless godless fear for our own
existence. From this fear arises a peculiar lack of fear, that has its seat
in all of us. Without fear that this might rebound upon ourselves we
seek to secure our life, our prosperity at the cost of others. Without
fear we seek profit, recking nothing of the loss of other peoples' lives.
Without fear we exploit other nations to increase our prosperity.
Today without fear we hear their cries of distress and accusations, since
as the weaker they cannot resist us. Without fear we build atomic
power-stations which with their poison will bring destruction only on
our successors. Without fear we obtain employment for workers and
profit through exporting arms, with which other people will tear each
other in pieces, or will be handed over to the mercies of their tyrants.
Without fear we stuff our countries with mass means of annihilation,
because, like fools, we believe that those in authority, with their small
cleverness have things so in control that we shall never be hoist with
our own petard. Without fear man is making life a hell, first for others,
and then for himself.

Often enough the revenge of the underdogs has struck back at those
in authority, who had imagined themselves to be secure from it. Yet
men do not learn from such experiences. Fear for their own existence
and their place in the sun makes men have no fear of their victims – and
no fear of God. And yet no other explanation can be given of the fact
that not only people who consider themselves atheists, and therefore
do not feel any compulsion to fear God, but also men living within the
sphere of Christianity, have incurred through the centuries, and still
more today the guilt of frightfully oppressing other men and waging
bloody wars, without fear of the God whom they worshipped in their
glittering cathedrals, whose word they heard, and whose Church they
paid. This God seemed to them harmless, weak and distant, only useful
to keep the underprivileged in check, and to prevent them from
retaliating.

This God, however, who wishes to speak his love to our hearts and to
the hearts of all men, this God declares himself to be an avenger of the
needy and the poor. (Proverbs 31, 9.) To him cries the blood of our
brother Abel, (Gen. 4, 10), and he hears it. It is not only the oppressed
who strike back; he strikes back, and I think that we Germans have
been given in our century a frightful lesson to this effect, one which we

have already almost forgotten. But the horizon of this intervention of God on behalf of the victims of our fearlessness is not confined to our earthly life. The guilt that we have incurred here through our action and neglect reaches beyond our death; the accusation will yet be made and paid for; for the cries of our victims, which we neglected and disregarded, will on the other side shrill threateningly in our ears, and we shall no longer be able to neglect or disregard them. This side of the biblical message may have become strange and unintelligible to us today. But that does not make it any less true, and that we neglect it is a sign of our Godforsakenness and our false lack of fear. When on the Day of Repentance in 1938, after the night of the Pogrom, we heard in the Dahlem Community Centre these words of the Baptist from the Lesson for today: "Ye brood of vipers! Who warned you to flee from the wrath to come?" (Luke 3, 7) we were stricken to the heart, and we knew what was coming on our people. We shall not escape "the wrath to come", not on earth, and if on earth we were to succeed, then we shall not escape it in the hereafter. God gives his commands for the protection of the weak. Where our manner of life, our economy and politics and armaments come up against this Protector of the weak, then our life is destroyed, dead, so dead as many men among us are already in their lust for money and power and armaments. And how deep this destruction goes we shall first see clearly when at last we stand in the light, the light of the eternal love of God. Because of this message we are compelled to make the Bible dumb, tear out its teeth; as has often effectively been done in Christendom, or persecute it, as I have just read in a newspaper account about Guatemala, a murderous land in which a murderous regime is held in power by the U.S.A. – and so with our support. "In this land" a priest reports, "Bibles are buried, because their possession is dangerous to life." Men are murdered without fear there and in El Salvador, and through fear of men, and without fear of God, our Bishops and the Pope are silent.

Fear of men, anxiety about one's own well-being, drives away the fear of God: the fear of God drives away the fear of men and anxiety about our own existence. The fear of God arises in us at the same time as joy and gratitude for the love of God. It is the fear not to stand on the side of the Protector of the weak, but against him on the side of the strong, who live at the cost of the weak. It is the fear of perhaps having the powerful of the world on our side, but God against us. This fear, says the Bible, "*is a source of life*". The word's intention is to allure us to see the enjoyment of life in a different light, not in the possession of wealth, which we grasp for ourselves, but in the grateful joy of those whom we can help with it. In the new relationships which are created when we do not enjoy our possessions for ourselves, but share them with those who are dependent on them. Such relationships, and such joy in life are often found among the dwellings of the poor, who can only survive because of their solidarity, rather than in the joyless homes of those who are possessed by their possessions. Imagine to yourselves that without the fear of man, of the Soviets, but in the fear of God we were to spend all the money used for armament on peaceful purposes, how we could thereby change the face of the earth! We would have overcome the catastrophe of hunger, we could create new relationships between the peoples, we could alter the life in our own land, even the snake-pits in our psychiatric clinics, for whose improvement once again the funds have been cancelled, while the spending on armaments remains untouched. We would have so altered our half of the world, that what seems to us reprehensible in Soviet Communism could no longer be dangerous to us. That may perhaps now seem utopian, we would have to speak about it earnestly. But what is utopia, and what is realism? From our belief that life according to God's will is utopian, and that a self-seeking life that protects itself with the weapons of death is realistic – we must be set free from that. It is this kind of realism that has brought the world today into the "bondage of death", to the edge of the abyss. Israel's word of wisdom says, realism of another kind! *"The fear of God is a source of life"*, and not a lack of fear in relation to God's will. The purpose of the word is to warn us and to teach us to see the true bondage of death.

In a recent discussion with many Tübingen students I mentioned the word of the philosopher Günter Anders in Vienna, who said that our motto for today must be "Make your neighbour anxious like yourself!" The students thought that there was enough fear, and that one ought not to increase it, and that nothing good came out of fear. But the Bible's purpose is in fact not merely to console us, but also to make us fear, to give us vision, so that we no longer mistake the bondage of death for our anchor of salvation, and to rise in revolt, even in the last moment, against the false fearlessness and the false safeguards of our life, which are in reality the bonds of death. We must convert to the true realism, made fearless by the true fear, the fear of God. The Gospel leads us from the anxious fear and the false fearlessness into the true fear of God. Let us enter the threatening year 1981 with the one fear that, without the fear of God, we might become more deeply entangled in the bonds of death which already envelope us, and with the prayer to him who teaches us the true fear and the true fearlessness, that he will transform us into fearless collaborators with the fear of God, of whom it is said in the Bible that he is not a lover of death, but a lover of life.